John Shebbeare

Letters on the English Nation

Vol. I

John Shebbeare

Letters on the English Nation
Vol. I

ISBN/EAN: 9783744689274

Printed in Europe, USA, Canada, Australia, Japan

Cover: Foto ©Thomas Meinert / pixelio.de

More available books at **www.hansebooks.com**

ON THE

ENGLISH NATION:

BY

BATISTA ANGELONI,

A JESUIT,

Who refided many years in LONDON.

Tranflated from the Original ITALIAN,

BY THE

AUTHOR of the MARRIAGE ACT a Novel.

Cupio in tantis reipublicæ periculis non diffolutum videri.   CICERO *in Catalinam.*

VOL. I.

LONDON:
Printed in the Year MDCCLV.

TO

The moſt high, puiſſant, and noble Prince * * * * * ,
Duke of * * * * * * ,
Marquis of * * * * * ,
&c. &c. &c. &c. &c. &c.

MY LORD,

THE pleaſure which attends this dedication to your Grace, is of ſo ſingular a nature, that very few writers, I imagine have ever poſſeſſed the like felicity. It is no leſs, my Lord, than a power of ſhewing how totally the letters of this papiſt which I have tranſlated, are diveſted of all foundation of truth, in the observations which they contain.

It is too frequently the hard fate of writers, my Lord, to be obliged to translate the works of authors which they do not approve, and contradict the sentiments of their hearts thro' a long work in every line which flows from their pen.

This, my Lord, tho' it may unhappily fall to my share, I cannot let pass unobserved, as too many British translators might have carelessly done: I intend therefore to shew with the best abilities, which so short a space will allow me, the falsities of his observations, by the recital of a very few of your Grace's virtues, actions, and excellencies; and thus oppose experience to speculation.

Yet, my Lord, I implore you to believe, that this design arises entirely from

a full

DEDICATION.

a full conviction of the truth of what I shall deliver; and not from any idea, partially entertained in your favour; at the same time I assure your Grace, that it does not spring from any base inclination of flattering you; the truth of which I am convinced you will have the goodness to believe before you have read thro' this address; but from a laudable desire of doing strict justice to your unparallell'd parts, and singular character, which I am fully assured no age has yet produced an equal to, and no future———; but let me not pretend to dive into the recesses of futurity, a sudden turn of thought towards the court of the heir apparent inclines me to believe, that your Grace may leave a successor equal to yourself in all the high arts, and accomplishments of governing.

In this dedication to your Grace, I am made peculiarly happy by the two most delectable ideas, which can attend

vi DEDICATION.

the human mind; the pleasure of doing you justice, in convincing the world of the errors, mistakes, and blunders, which this papist has asserted, and giving ease to my own conscience, which would not permit me to sleep in peace, till I had declared to you and my country, the true difference which exists between my manner of thinking, and that of the original author.

This dedication, however, I implore your Grace to receive as an hasty sketch of some future design, and not as any thing pretended to be finished; as a hint of what people ought to think of you, rather than a description of your full glories; something that my heart pants to complete with all possible truth and expedition; so, that there may not remain a single doubt in any one breast of this island, of the real extent of your capacity, and of the true use which you have proved to your country in peace and war.

ONE

DEDICATION.

ONE of the first assertions of this catholic writer, my Lord, is, That the Whig idea, of every man's possessing a right of deciding for himself in matters of religion, is destructive of true liberty, and must, from the love of power so natural to man, terminate, in making a minister absolute.

NOTHING is so apt to deceive, my Lord, as speculative reasoning; the web of which is finely spun from arguments à priori, where men pretend to draw from causes those consequences which experience teaches us are never to be found in the sequel: in this manner was this author deceived.

BUT permit me, my Lord, without suspicion of adulation, to draw a most illustrious instance of this truth from the beha-

behaviour of your Grace, and many other conspicuous Whigs.

CAN it ever be forgotten, my Lord, by the ——— and people of England, with what amazing modesty, resignation, and humility, your Grace, accompanied with many other complete Whigs, offered to resign into the hands of your Master, all the high offices, posts, charges, honors, and advantages you enjoy'd, in preference of one superior understanding, which he intended to take to his councils.

IN this, did you not gloriously determine to sacrifice all private interest, and relinquish all particular advantage? And this, my Lord, at a time when rebellion was in the land, your master engaged in a war on the continent, and the money-jobbers of the city refused to lend the supplies to every one but you, even at this instant when it was scarce possible for his
——— to

―――― to displace you. Such was the consciousness of your own worth, obedience to your Master, and promotion of your country's weal, that you would unanimously have surrendered all posts, honors and profits into his hands, on the account of one man, universally acknowledged of greater understanding.

Can such astonishing resignation, and disinterested actions, spring from the love of power? shall Whigs hereafter be stigmatized with arbitrary dispositions, when no reign can produce one instance of equal humility and subjection in a minister?

Thus, my Lord, this single instance is sufficient to demonstrate the falsehood of this papist's assertion; it proves that the practice of a Whig manifestly contradicts his speculative conceptions; that humility, modesty, resignation, and duty, are the effects

x DEDICATION.

effects of those causes and principles, which he afferted would generate pride, arrogance, disobedience, and usurpation. Here, my Lord, give me leave to rejoyce with you, in producing this happy proof of experience, which so thoroughly clears you and all Whigs, from the malicious infinuations that are contained in this popish author; since the first annals of the British empire, it could never be said with so much truth as at present, The king can do no wrong.

With what piety does your Grace preserve gray hairs, and declining life, from that fatigue which attends looking into public affairs; and dispose of all things without disturbing the quiet of his days? With what wonderful invention do you devise means to keep that intelligence which would displease him, from his eyes, and lull him with tales of more amusing circumstances?

The

THE care and pain of diſtributing all things, either honorary, or lucrative, your Grace has ſo prudently eaſed your Maſter's hands of, that in all the late changes and appointments of his ſervants, the very letters which compoſe his title, were never heard amongſt the people.

IT is ſaid, his Grace has given the poſt of **** to the honourable ****; the office of **** to the right honorable *****; the garter to the moſt high and puiſſant ****. So tender are you in troubling his repoſe; thus are you at once the nurſe of *****, and people grown old and paſt the vigor of their lives.

NOR is the ———— alone indebted to your Grace for the immenſe care you have ſhewn, in exonerating his ſhoulders of the weight of reigning; did not his ſon prove an equal inſtance of your attention,

to

xii   DEDICATION:

to his eafe alfo? with the moft becoming modefty you decently contrived to fupplant him at that univerfity, over which he wifhed to prefide; even contrary to his will you procured yourfelf to be elected head of that place, and bravely dared his difpleafure, to fave him from the trouble which attends fuch a charge? Can the prefent fon forget your affection for his departed fire? Can you fail of continued honors from him, who have thus alike politely treated his father and grand-father? Will he not hereafter fhew his fenfe of thefe proceedings? How ridiculous then to affert, that the prefent adminiftration of affairs requires the principles of a Tory, to preferve the king's prerogative, and peoples rights, from the ambitious views of a Whig-adminiftration.

IN matters relating to religion, my Lord, give me leave to obferve, that this author is equally miftaken, as he is in
thofe

DEDICATION. xiii

those of the Whig-principles. But when we consider him as a papist, bred under the darkness of Jesuitism, in a land of slavery and church-despotism, imbibing prejudices from infancy by this education; it is not much to be wonder'd at, that the paths which you pursue in policy should be incomprehensible to his circumscribed conception.

Religion, my Lord, may be allowed in Italy, in a land of arbitrary power; it may form one part of government where men are born slaves, composed of all the depreciating faculties and passions, that disgrace human nature: in that country indeed, the belief of a God, and of future rewards and punishments, may be of public utility, and necessary to influence the lives of the inhabitants.

But in Britain, a land of liberty, where the innocent natives are almost returned to a state of nature, can a man be said to be truly free, whose dastard soul dreads the offending his creator; or, who is harrassed by the slavish apprehensions of punishment in another world, for actions which his constitution continually prompts him to commit in this.

How ought we then to congratulate each other, that such humiliating tenets have been totally extirpated during your administration? Right reason, the love of virtue, moral rectitude, and the fitness of things, are the sole motives which influence the nobler parts of a Briton's mind: you alone are the terror of the guilty.

In all commercial states, my Lord, it has been ever allowed the distinguishing mark of a legislator and statesman, to encourage those kinds of commerce, where the original materials are of the least worth, and the chief value of the commodities arises from the labour of the people; in this

DEDICATION. xv

this art, your Grace, and your immortal predeceſſor, have excelled all the ſons of men. You have created a gainful merchandize without labour, from materials of no value.

To inſtance in one reſpect only; what was the ſingle article of conſcience worth in this kingdom, before your adminiſtration? the utmoſt that could be ſaid in favour of the beſt was, that it gave a man a chearful countenance, and made his ſlumbers ſweet and eaſy. But, did it ſate the hungry appetite, or clothe the naked limbs of virtue in diſtreſs? Of what uſe was it then to the poſſeſſor?

Since your prudential, and virtuous adminiſtration, how conſpicuous is the change? Not a little borough remains in England, where the very worſt of all conſciences may not be ſold once in ſeven years, for what is ſufficient to ſuſtain a moderate family during that time; of ſuch increaſed value has that trifle been made thro' all England, during your superintendance of the nation's welfare; and tho' your Grace cannot be said to be the first dealer in this commodity, to your immortal honor it must be allowed, that you have more than trebled its value, since you have taken it under your protection, and voluntarily condescended to be constantly chosen master of that company which are the greatest traders in that merchandize.

How great then are the obligations which starving virtue owes to your charitable disposition? What thanks are due to such public spiritedness, and care for poverty in distress? When will the stupid people repay you as you deserve?

Nor is your public-spirited disposition confined to this country alone; the neighbouring isle, which depends on this kingdom, has felt the auspicious influence; the judicious protection which you gave

to

DEDICATION. xvii

to a certain favorite, has created such a marvellous spirit of patriotism, as cannot be equalled in all ancient story; what floods of claret have been exhausted in loyal healths to his majesty, by this your prudent management? To what degree must a minister be loved, when one single action can produce such an universal spirit of patriotism in a nation? Would you not suspect me of adulation, if I should deliver my real sentiments to your Grace? Can such a people ever be tempted to revolt against this darling minister?

YET to your eternal fame, this spirit rests not there: the commands which have been given to the governors of the British plantations, particularly New-York, have created an equal esteem for you in that country; the singular mildness of expression in their speeches; and the sacredness, with which you observed your promises made, during the last war, have united the inhabitants universally in one

Vol I.   b   passion,

passion, sentiment, and opinion towards you. There is scarce an island or colony where the British power presides, which is not filled with admiration of the governors you send, and of you who send them. Never was there an union at home and abroad, in the judgment of all ranks and degrees, concerning the ministerial abilities of any man, equal to that which is to be found in their opinions of your Grace.

How thankfully will the Americans receive the twelve-hundred soldiers, which you are sending to their aid? How equal to the task of destroying the settlements of Canada and Mississippi, is this military force? Which, considering the superiority of British courage, and skill of its officers, to those of France, and that the French are but ten thousand seven-hundred regular troops (not quite ten to one); what probability is there that they can look us in the face, and how feasable is the project of driving them out of the American continent?

INDEED,

INDEED, my Lord, the Americans are a hard-headed and stubborn race, descended from those fathers, who are great enemies to ministers; they have shewn in the late wars that they dare to fight, and will follow no leaders but those born in their own country: for this reason it may be presumed you have sent them officers from this kingdom, left being innured to martial affairs under their own countrymen, they may declare themselves independent.

By this single thought you have fully contrived, that they shall raise no army, and thrown the blame on the planters, who will not inlist under the natives of England.

THUS you have preserved yourself from all impeachment of neglect, in succouring the Americans, prevented a war, and given no umbrage to the French government.

THIS appears to me the moſt machievilian and refined ſtretch of all human policy.

NOTHING, my Lord, is ſo common amongſt men of feeble ûnderſtanding, as to form judgments, and found prejudices on the maxims and manners of their illuſtrious anceſtors; becauſe Horace, Juvenal, and other ancient Greek, and Latin writers of immortal honor, exclaimed againſt informers as the moſt deteſted race of men, they would infer, that your attention to theſe miſcreants, is highly culpable.

BUT alas! ſuch is their ſhort-ſighted ken into your policy, ſo abſolutely different from that of Minos, Solon, Lycurgus, and Numa, thoſe drivelers in the old ſyſtems of government, that they do not perceive

one

DEDICATION.

one excellence in your new and unprecedented manner of governing.

WILL any man dare to condemn this inclination in your Grace, who has heard of that bloody rebellion so destructive to this nation, which was carried on by three drunken boys in the university of Oxford; or of that plot, which makes every christian's blood run cold with horror at the recital of it; that horrid plot, which was like to prove so destructive to all England, because it was so secretly conducted, so secretly concealed in rags, that all men of sense believe, it had never been discovered but for him that invented it; can such discoverers be denominated informers, too well rewarded, or too highly distinguished? Can you be too much adored, for thus watching over the sleeping nation.

YET, give me leave to observe, that this malicious papistical author, has not

DEDICATION.

penetrated into the true defign of your Grace; in this behaviour, no man has manifefted more indignation againft thefe pefts of fociety than yourfelf.

Your Grace knows as well as any man living (being moft extremely profound in the knowledge of paft and prefent hiftory, the manners of ancient and modern kingdoms, and the fyftems of all former legiflators) that it has ever been the undeviating cuftom for all honeft men to confider fuch traiterous and degenerate beings, as fellows branded in the forehead with the infamous mark of information.

This then muft of confequence make them detefted, and fhun'd by all honeft company. The felon, burnt in the hand, bears that ftigma, which muft for ever prevent his being employed by all virtuous people; thus obliged to continue the fame impious employment, at laft the gallows

gallows terminates his illuſtrious race of glory.

In like manner the informer, deteſted and excluded from all virtuous ſociety, marked in his face by the feelings of his conſcience, muſt naturally have wanted bread, and continued in the ſame execrable employ, if your ſuperlative prudence had not placed him above neceſſity; and thus charitably, virtuouſly, honorably, conſcientiouſly, and chriſtianly, prevented him from all future inclination to treachery and information. How exalted then is your conception in this inſtance of refined policy? How effectually are theſe miſcreants withheld from all future inſidious deſigns againſt their fellow-creatures? How abſolutely are all others diſcouraged from attempting the like baſeneſs, leſt like too many of late, they ſhould be exalted to ſome high ſtation, and thus become a conſpicuous and flagrant object of the public ſcorn? How new, un-

DEDICATION.

common, and decisive is this your manner of suppressing this execrable race of informers!

MINISTERS, my Lord, have frequently met with unsuitable returns from the people, whose happiness they superintended; but no one has ever received usage so unequal to his deserts, as your Grace: your eye, ever watchful over the morals and religion of the subjects, (witness the many laws, which have been made in their favour during your administration) could not behold the declining cause of Christ without much secret very secret grief, and repining; instigated by this decay, you piously determined to recall the languishing state of christianity, by intending intimately to mix the Jews, the chosen people of heaven, with this nation. What sanguine hopes did this beget of restoring the christian religion? How would morality have been improved by this race, so remarkable

for

DEDICATION.

for the strict observance of it all over Europe?

THIS law, which was to give them the civil rights of christians, to encourage their coming hither, in your harangues you insisted to be of the utmost public utility; you told us, it was made to mend the people, and then you said it was revoked to please the people; it was created with vigor, because it was a most excellent law, and it was suddenly abrogated, because it was never proved to the contrary: how refined is this policy! how convincing is the manner of reasoning! new and unknown to our mole-eyed ancestors; how few mortals can discern your exquisite designs in civil institutions?

ANOTHER law, my Lord, has also with equal injustice been exclaimed against; it is that, which has been made against clandestine marriage.

SHALL

DEDICATION.

SHALL young people, my Lord, actuated with the paſſions which God only has given them, be permitted to chuſe partners for life, becauſe they love each other, and it is a matter which relates chiefly to their happineſs? Where then is the wiſdom which grey hairs afford to age, and the diſcretion which ſeventy imparts to judgments in love-affairs, when they no longer taſte the leaſt remain of that ſeductive paſſion?

IN this, my Lord, this author has been equally miſtaken, as in all his former remarks; he does not conceive, that miniſters are obliged too frequently to diſguiſe their true deſigns from vulgar eyes and common obſervation, to make one object paſs for another, and conceal truth by ſpecious appearances.

IT has been too long, my Lord, a juſt complaint, that the inferior clergy of this land

DEDICATION. xxvii

land starved in learning, penury, and neglect, whilst the unlettered and dignified wallowed in pleasure and excess; that the pious and humane curate, who officiated in his duty with decency, was scarce clothed as he ought; his rector, like Dives, faired sumptuously every day, clad in fine linnen.

This complaint, by one superior stroke, is at last effectually removed by this piously intended law; the distressed curates will all speedily be provided for in America, and incumbents obliged to do their duty themselves: thus, there will no more remain that object of reproach on those, who have neglected the clergy.

But, my Lord, it was necessary to conceal this your intention for the established clergy, from the jealous eyes of presbyterians, lest this kindness, so partially shewn to them, should wean their affections from you,

you, which you are conscious they always withdrew on the least neglect, and thus deprive you of that kind of assistance, which is not to be expected from those of the established religion. With what address was this your pious design disguised in this law? How apparently does it prove, that the established church, and her sons are your peculiar care!

NEVER since the beginning of things, was there a more unjust allegation against man, than this which has been asserted, that you are an enemy to liberty. When alas! so true is the contrary of this assertion, that there are public assemblies permitted and undisturbed, where full liberty is allowed to dispute the existence of that God which forms the object of the national religion.

YE ingrates, how can this allegation proceed from your lips? is not this a liberty unknown,

DEDICATION.

unknown, and unallowed in any nation, pagan or chriſtian, to this day.

How can it be aſſerted, that your Grace intends to deſtroy liberty, who have given no bounds to it? How can you be ſaid to be the enemy of the chriſtian religion, who have allowed ſuch freedom in ſearching into its truths?

Indeed (your Grace will pardon this ſeeming flattery) you reſemble your Creator in nothing, ſo much as in that liberty which was firſt given to our parents in Eden, to eat of the fruit of all trees but one; in like manner, free liberty is given to pluck from the ——— religion, laws, public and private property and character; the tree of knowledge was the only interdicted thing in Paradiſe; the examination of your policy, in Britain; two things which, tho' totally unlike, are yet my Lord, equally myſtical and inexplicable: can

this

this single reſtriction be deemed a breach of liberty?

My Lord, there are many which accuſe you with ſtrange deſigns againſt your country's welfare: ſurely nothing was ever done with equal injuſtice; I am convinced that it would be extremely eaſy for me to prove, that you have been totally void of all deſign, thro' the whole tenour of your adminiſtration; your very enemies the French, have ever been ſtrictly convinced of this truth.

And here, my Lord, I ſpeak from certain knowledge, and therefore, the more boldly aſſert, that no Britiſh miniſter ever poſſeſſed an equal intereſt in the opinion of the French king and his miniſtry; nay, ſuch is the regard which they profeſs for you, that ſhould any popular attempt remove you from your maſter's ear and council, I am thoroughly convinced, that not only the moſt chriſtian king, but his whole court, would unite in one petition for your being

DEDICATION.

being restored to his favour, and your honors; such interesting impression you have created in the hearts of your very enemies: your presents are the most acceptable, of all those which arrive at Belle Veue; the marchioness never fails of smiling at the mention of your name, your actions afford the subject of many a pleasant conversation, between this lady and her royal lover; she dignifies you with the name of the most christian minister, who having been smitten on one cheek, have turned to them, she says, the other also; nay, a story of you will create a laugh of approbation, in the most melancholy hours of his majesty, when every other attempt has proved abortive; such is your power and interest, in the nation of our natural enemies.

IT is a melancholy consideration, my Lord, that men in high stations can no more avoid the scourge of calumny, than they can exist without food; it is therefore

fore the more to be admired, that so little a share has fallen on your Grace. The Tories are eternally exclaiming against the inattention which you have shewn to forming a militia, and this Papistical author has joined in the clamour.

But, my Lord, in this instance, as in all the preceding, they do not penetrate your true design, and manner of governing; shall the brave peasants of Britain conceive, because they are naked and unarmed, that they are not a match for the regular troops of the French monarch? Shall we free born English, intimate the least appearance of timidity? what ill-judged temerity would that be, which the Tories call prudence? should your Grace arm and discipline the peasants of this land, would not this mistaken prudence be construed by the French, as an apprehension of an invasion from that nation, and consequently, would they not invade us thus armed

and

DEDICATION.

and equipt, becaufe of thefe tokens of fear; this they will never dare to attempt, whilft they fee us unarmed and unafraid? What rafhnefs then, to confefs fuch daftard difpofitions, by providing ourfelves with arms, and thus, as it were challenging them to invade us.

BESIDES, my Lord, the great excellence of a minifter is, to be thoroughly acquainted with the manners, and way of thinking, of thofe nations with whom he is engaged; the indifputed characteriftic of the French nation is politenefs; will thefe polite people then violate that character, and come hither armed, to a nation that is difarmed, and in no condition to receive them? or, if we fhould arm ourfelves, would not they immediately, actuated by the fame polite fpirit, pay us a vifit becaufe we feem to be prepared to receive them as we ought.

THIS, my Lord, is another aftonifhing inftance of that uncommon penetration, which you abound in above all men, a fample of that exquifitely curious manner of governing, and faving the nation's money, abfolutely unknown to our thick-fighted anceftors; the kingdom is fafe from all invafions, from the nature of our enemies, why then a military power to prevent an invafion which cannot happen? Thus you have moft admirably tranfmuted that which has been hitherto farcaftically ftyled the moft palpable neglect, into the moft refined policy, a policy, my Lord, equally refined and perfpicuous in all its parts, with this laft inftance that I have mentioned.

THERE is yet another imputation againft your Grace, which, with his ufual injuftice, this writer has thrown upon you; it is my Lord, the inattention which you
have

have shewn, towards providing for men of genius and learning. My Lord, I can produce almost numberless instances of the great provision which you have made for the most stupid, unlettered, and worthless of God's creation; can it be conceived then, that this can arise from any thing, but ignorance where true merit is to be found? if your Grace could discover where it lyes, is it to be imagined, that informers would be preferred to men of honor, the sons of dullness to those of genius, vice to virtue, impudence to modesty, deceit to integrity, irreligion to piety? with what injustice then is this imputed as a crime to your Grace, who are by nature and situation, out of all power of distinguishing the difference. Can any man who shines so eminently, in all the parts of a minister, be so deficient in this of a man, unless the true distinction of merit and demerit, was totally concealed from him?

DEDICATION.

IF there be any one thing, my Lord, in which the works of the author which I have tranflated, feem to coincide with the conduct of your adminiftration, it is in the following inftances :

THAT the regal power in future times, may poffible become too feeble, and religion lofe its influence thro' neglect of external objects, which may ftrongly actuate the minds of men.

IN confequence of this opinion, it may be humbly prefumed, that men who are known to acquiefce in favour of thefe fentiments, are made the fuperintendants of the ——— of ——— and the reft of the ——— ——— How miraculoufly provident are you in all things! you fee into diftant futurity with the fame perfpicuity, that you behold thofe objects which are prefent to your eyes.

DEDICATION.

THESE, my Lord, and a thousand other instances I could produce, equally convincing how much your ministerial judgment is to be admired, beyond all that has ever been found in the administration of former statesmen; your wars conducted, and peace concluded, in a manner the most amazing to all Europe; your skill in encouraging trade by promoting public companies; your increasing the national wealth by making paper equal in value with gold, the former of which we are not likely to want, and may remain in this land, after every dust of the latter is exported to Germany, and the East Indies.

THUS, my Lord, I hope that I have advanced a great way towards reconciling the minds of those who have been mistaken, into one opinion of you; and shewn, how truly your administration differs from the remarks of this blinded Papist.

YET

YET as it is probable, my Lord, tho' this may have great influence on your friends, that your enemies may still persist in their obstinacy of opinion, regarding your Grace; I intend to shew the true and essential difference between the times of Charles the first and the present, between the then Lord Strafford and your Grace; draw a comparison of his understanding and your Grace's, your virtues and his, his ministerial conduct and yours, the crimes imputed to him and you, the disposition of Englishmen at that time and at present, your parliamentary knowledge and that of that nobleman, the taxes levied then and now, and shew the national incumbrance at each time: thro' the whole examination I shall endeavour to strip off the delusive surface, which covered the kingdom at that period, and compare it nakedly and impartially with this; and then analizing the different times and manners, the causes of

applause

applause and resentment, the falsehood of his and truth of your administration, endeavour to assign the true reasons which may justify a nation in executing a minister.

IN the execution of this design, I must necessarily bring before the public eye, the past conduct of your Grace's life; and then I make no doubt that every man from the comparison will be truly convinced of the essential difference which exists between you, and render your Grace exactly that applause which you merit.

As a lover of my country I cannot refuse myself this satisfaction; besides this, my Lord, the singular favour with which you have distinguished me, in taking such particular and partial notice of my small performance, and letting the works and the editor of the great Lord Bolingbroke, so truly calculated for private good, and public welfare, pass unobserved and unnoticed

DEDICATION.

ticed by you, is what a grateful mind can never forget.

THERE remains, my Lord, that I befeech your Grace to believe, that in this future defign, I fhall endeavour to abftain from all appearance of adulation; that I fhall give you no reafon to blufh from remarks too partially made in your favour; that I fhall reprefent facts as they are, and yet praife you as you deferve.

INDEED, this dedication by many of your enemies, may feem to contradict this defign of preferving impartiality, and create a fufpicion even in your Grace, that the fpirit of flattery may enter too much into my future writings; but, my Lord, as thofe I have confulted on this head agree in the truth of all that is here intended, why fhould your enemies and your Grace's modefty withhold me from the truth?

IF

IF a war then should unhappily be declared, how great will be my pleasure to be engaged, from time to time, in placing your management in its true light? exhibit to the public attention, your magnanimity and ministerial capacity, in the most conspicuous point of view; your labours for the national welfare, and neglect of your own; and thus excite this discontented people to their duty, and justly point out how you ought to be considered by them?

BUT, my Lord, before I take my leave of you in this dedication, let me entreat you to forgive the liberty I am going to take; do not conceive that it arises from any imagined or visionary deficiency in your Grace; I implore you to believe me, that nothing but your own and the nation's welfare, could possibly have drawn this request from my bosom; will you then have the infinite goodness to pardon me in
this

DEDICATION.

this requeſt? tho' it may appear extremely ſingular in its kind, I am confident your Grace will indulge me in it, for the good of that nation which you are ſo watchful over; it is, may it pleaſe you, moſt noble and puiſſant prince, That you would condeſcend, for the eaſe of your adminiſtration and the people's good, to permit that moſt eminent and ſciehtific, tho' too much neglected calculator, ſtateſman, and friend to Britain, Jacob Henriques, to fill ſome poſt of high importance near your perſon; his ſkill in paying the nation's debts, and raiſing money without any one's contributing a ſhilling towards it, will certainly be moſt extremely uſeful in times of war, tho' it muſt be avowed your method, by reducing money to no value, is new and admirable.

CONSIDER then, may not caſh fail and paper become ſuſpected, if you proceed in this war as in the laſt; let me then

DEDICATION.

then entreat your Grace, to take him to your's and the nation's aid; it is not to be imagined, what aſtoniſhing advantages may redound to this kingdom, from an union of two ſuch inimitable and comprehenſive underſtandings; his ſaving and your directing ſpirit, mixed with ſuch probable and extenſive ſcheming, will without doubt complete the happineſs of this iſle, already ſo greatly advanced by your Grace's peculiar management.

I HAVE, my Lord, already, from the little knowledge I have in the works of art, deſigned the frontiſpiece which is to accompany my future productions on your Grace; the following lines, my Lord, are a deſcription of it.

BY this your Grace, who I am credibly informed are to the full as knowing in the works of art, as in thoſe of government, and decide as juſtly of the merits of pictures

xliv DEDICATION.

tures as of men, will have sufficient time to steal a moment from the nation's care, consider of the design before it be carried into execution, and make alterations, if any shall be found neceſſary.

IN the fore-ground your Grace is placed beneath a canopy on a throne, in just attitude, and full expreſſion of that wonderful understanding, steady behaviour, becoming grace, and true importance, which you so eminently poſſeſs, and which have so long done honor to this nation, in the opinion of all foreign ministers.

THE favourite bird of wisdom, the sagacious owl, always busied in the dark, perched like the pigeon of Mahomet on your shoulder, whispers your most prudent counsels, his tail is turned towards the people of England, from which part during his communication with your Grace, a certain species of matter drops upon your
George

DEDICATION.

George and Garter, at once an emblem of your being advised, beloved, and rewarded, by that great goddess Minerva.

BEFORE your feet sits Britannia become twi-child, playing with the cap of folly, which she mistakes for that of liberty.

BEHIND you in a nitch, stands the figure of one of the kings of England made of wax.

ON the left hand, a little retired, parents at your command are binding their children in chains, and the Presbyterian teachers, armed with thong-whips, driving the necessitous clergy in tattered crape, fettered together like hounds in couples, on board ships which lye ready to transport them to America; religion, beauty, and innocence in tears, implore in vain to save them from this treatment.

ON

DEDICATION.

ON your right hand is a large group of puppets, which are so constructed, that on your Grace's pulling a string, the puppet you intend rises up, with open mouth, to speak whatever you shall dictate.

THESE with many emblematical devices, form the frontispiece of the work in which I intend to do justice to your Grace.

IF it shall have the happiness to find favour in your eyes, it will add to that pleasure which I already possess, in subscribing myself,

May it please your Grace,

your Grace's most obedient,

most dutiful, most humble,

and most devoted servant.

The TRANSLATOR.

PREFACE.

THE many lives of authors which have been written, sufficiently evince the natural desire that people entertain, of knowing the particulars which relate to men of letters; to satisfy this curiosity, the Translator has determined to give some account of the person, who wrote the following epistles.

THE author Batista Angeloni was a Roman by birth, and bred at Rome in the college of that religious order, which is called the jesuits; during his studies he applied himself closely to the understanding, amongst other languages, that of the English; the authors which he read, created in him a great inclination to see the nation which had produced them; he therefore came to this kingdom as a missionary, and resided many years in London, and it is but very lately that those, whether of his persuasion, or of a different, who knew and loved him, have been

been robbed by death of that pleasure which was the constant attendant of his company, and which is most sincerely regretted.

His figure was pleasing, his face expressive, particularly his eye, his manners engaging; he remarked the objects of sense, and felt those of sensation with singular accuracy, and tenderness, and was much more just in his reasoning, than correct in his style; he had great quickness in conceiving the truth of things intuitively, and was not always patient enough to explain it to men of slower apprehension; of a satyric turn in conversation against polite and unpolite vice; in secret the most humane, compassionate, and tender to all human failings and distress.

His chief excellence consisted in analizing the human mind, discovering the most active and prevalent faculties in our composition, adapting proper objects to each, and distinguishing the motives to actions in men; by long application and delight in this kind of study, he possest an insight into the nature of man, beyond what is to be found but in very few of the species.

FROM

FROM this particular turn, and natural perspicuity, he beheld human nature as it is, divested of that exalted idea which the present deistical reasoners affect to compliment it with, and yet not so depreciated and base, as the wild and extravagant humility of the Presbyterian and Methodist delights to conceive and assert it to be.

HE had much compared his own particular mind with those of others, and had long concluded that the same principles were in all, but vastly different in degree; and that from the inequality of faculties in each, arose in great part the variety which is found in human kind; a passion which is weak in one, is often strong in another: in like manner the perfection of the senses, the delicacy of internal feelings, the powers of the imagination, the strength of reasoning, the promptness of faith, were all variously proportioned, and yet to be found in some degree in all; from this he inferred, that as the human mind was compounded of all these distinct faculties, that objects were originally created for each faculty, and that the true legislator ought to adapt those

PREFACE.

which were the moſt agreeable to the nature of man, and conducive to the general welfare.

IN all inſtitutions civil and religious, it was his ſtanding maxim, that the ſenſes, paſſions, faith, imagination, and reaſon, ought to be influenced by objects, which are proper to incite the mind to virtue, and withhold it from vice.

FROM a full conviction of this truth, he ſuſtained, that nothing had in it ſo little reaſon, as that pretenſion of the Deiſts to govern mankind by reaſon, excluding the objects of faith, and the influence of religion; and that examining the individual articles of a nation's religious belief, by the inquiſition of reaſon, according to the preſent deiſtical writers, was the moſt infallible mark of a limited and narrow underſtanding, unpractiſed in human nature, and blind to its conduct in mental proceeding; in religious conſiderations, he never diſtinguiſhed between utility and truth; whatever then was uſeful, in his opinion was true; and this, eſtabliſhed by law, made national truth; for this reaſon he entertained the moſt contemptible opinion of Chub above all writers: the mind, ſays he, diveſted of

a rea religious faith established by law, will adopt a more absurd one in its place, and become more ridiculous by the change; it is my constant remark, that none give credit to such absurdities, as those who pretend to believe nothing.

Utility and truth in all national conduct, whether civil or religious, being the same thing in his opinion; he concluded that whoever intended to diminish the influence of religious ordinances on the mind of man, was either weak or wicked, and consequently destructive of the public good; for this reason, a certain bishop, who has endeavoured to set the human mind loose from every anchor which can hold it steady to virtue, into the open, stormy ocean of infidelity and private opinion, was no great favourite of his.

His rule of right and wrong, truth or falsehood, in the institution and objects for moral and religious obligation, was the fitness and propriety which they bore to the faculties existing in the human mind; and from this way of conceiving things, he always insisted that no system of philosophy or religion, ancient or modern, or union of both, so truly corresponded to the whole composition of man in head and heart, as the christian religion: this I imagine will appear in his letters.

From this sagacity in considering the human powers, he had also seen the necessity of each faculty being animated and restrained, by motives which are native and original to it; for this reason he entertained the most despicable opinion of the ministry who presided in public affairs, who had weakly imagined, that money was a proper incentive to honorable actions in war, and that men could be purchased by it, to virtuous and becoming deeds. In their whole administration, he frequently asserted, that not the least ray of the knowledge of mankind, appeared thro' the darkness of their conduct; and in consequence of this, that every nation, so directed, must necessarily tumble into ruin.

There seem but very few men in nature of understanding sufficiently perfect to make reasonable and just observations on the actions of human nature, in the different manners, customs,

and

and laws of nations; of these again how few can divest themselves of original and invisible prejudices, which they have imbibed from education and manners of their own country, and justly distinguish between right and wrong, in those comparisons which they make between the religion, laws, constitution, and government of other nations and their own?

THE institutions in religion and government in the land we are born, generally constitute the idea of right in these things, in the minds of the individuals, and most men consider these as fixed rules of truth to try others by, rather than as objects to be examined by what is to be found in other nations; and even those of a more liberal manner of conceiving things, cannot divest themselves of that education which has influenced all their lives, and formed their manner of thinking, sufficiently to judge impartially, between the fitness or unfitness of a government, in all parts, to the original fabric of the human mind.

BESIDES this, that partial love of our country, which tho' it ought to enter strongly into every

every heart, should be as strenuously excluded from the head of every examiner of national institutions, is very apt to disguise the truth, and secret it from ourselves.

LIKE children, the natives are blind to the faults, and magnifiers of the virtues, which are inherent in their mother country; the sanguine mind exalting every virtue, conceives his nation the supreme of all, and invincible; the timid, uniting fear with love, is aghast at every apprehension of an attack from abroad, and trembles for his country; each of these from their native constitutions, where passions are strongly united with reason, are equally biassed to different and fallacious opinions, no true observation is to be expected from these men; and yet such form the generality of all nations. Thus then, a true state of any kingdom is not to be expected from the natives, either in its domestic police, or foreign influence; for the same reason that the English are prohibited from seeing their national customs in a true light, strangers are equally prevented by their prepossession in their own favour; besides this, they

seldom

PREFACE.

seldom tarry long enough in any country, to wear off the prevalency of first impressions, to be intimately acquainted with a people's manners, accustomed to their habits, and uninfluenced from particular prejudices.

IF ever they remain in any kingdom long enough to effectuate all this, they bid fairest to discover the real situation of it, to weigh its policy and religion with that of others, and draw the least partial conclusions.

To know one country well, it is necessary to have long resided in some other; the medium which forms itself in the mind of man habituated to reflexion, cannot settle into the center of things, without being weaned from old customs by the habit of new; the loss on one side, and gain on the other, bring the ballance as near as possible to an equipoise.

IF this be acceded to, the writer of the following letters promises some appearance of truth in his remarks; his long-living in this island had weaned him from former prejudice, and even created a love for its inhabitants; it is to be

hoped

hoped therefore, that the following remarks are neither trifling, inaccurate, prejudiced, or unjuſt; of this the reader will decide. The friends of the author thought them worth giving to the public, and at their requeſt they are tranſlated, yet not without permiſſion granted by him during his indiſpoſition; from his hands I received them in the Italian, and from mine they go to the public in Engliſh: I had once an inclination to have printed them in the original, but the bookſeller imagined an edition in that language, would not be diſpoſed of.

There is this farther to be objected on this head, that the author, being a catholic, may be imagined to incline too much to that manner of thinking in religion and government; it muſt however, at the ſame time be remembered, that we are Proteſtants, and not under leſs influence of prejudice and education, than thoſe who are bred in nations of more arbitrary power, and more ceremonious worſhip; that if being educated under the influence of fear from churchmen and ſtateſmen, may depreſs the mind, being brought up unchecked by either of theſe reſtraints,

PREFACE. lvii

restraints, lets loose the soul into all that is wild and extravagant; in short, that whatever can be said against men so bred, may in another view be opposed against us who are not; so that neither can be a proper judge of what each country truly is, whilst the individuals continue under the influence of their original education.

If this man originally possessed the effect of his youthful prejudices, in the pursuit and attention of his later studies he lost them; not worn into deism by disapproving all religion, nor blown into extravagant enthusiasm by contemning reason; examination had made him drop from the vast pomp and parade of popery, and despise the pretended simplicity of Quakers and Presbyterians; if he saw that the mind of men might be too much busied in ceremony, and thence neglect the real duties of religious worship, he was convinced also, that in its nature it was not susceptible of that purity, and simplicity, affected by the sectaries; he observed, that a false and exorbitant faith was the consequence of the first, and hypocrisy, detestable vice, the effect of the other; and that human nature, to be well directed, must be influenced by objects justly

adapted

adapted in nature and degree to every faculty in the soul. This was his syftem of natural government; as a man of honor, he did not choofe to change the manner of profeffing his religion; as a chriftian, he confidered vows made in that awful view, as indelible; as a philofopher, he beheld things in another light, where no one mode appearing perfect, the difference was not fufficient to create a renunciation of former tenets; laftly, his fixed opinion was, that chriftianity contained in itfelf the moft perfect of all philofophies.

The following letters being all written fome time fince, it is to be hoped, that no one will apply perfonally what they contain, from any imaginary refemblance which may be found between thofe who were then in the adminiftration, and thefe who have at prefent this honor; if they fhould be guilty of this miftake, it is they and not the author, who are to be blamed in that application.

If there fhould appear any feeming contradictions in this collection, it may be offered in defence of that appearance, that a man is not

lefs

PREFACE. lix

less different from himself at some times, than two men are different from each other; that every faculty has its hour of reigning, and that objects appear extremely different to the same mind, according to the medium thro' which they are seen; the gay and gloomy minutes have not a less influence on objects, than sun-shine and shade, and the man of to-day, looking at things thro' one disposition, approves what another day's review may condemn beheld thro' a different temper: hope gilds the objects of one hour, and fear obscures the same considered on the next.

In this manner things might have been beheld by the author of these letters; nay, perhaps, this very particular circumstance may render them more generally pleasing, as variety of dispositions may find something to like and disapprove, the latter of which has its pleasure in many heads, and even contradictory minds by approving and condemning in direct opposition to each other.

To be agreeable to all, is, in the nature of things, impossible; and the author is removed

from

PREFACE.

from all possible power of suffering from invective; tho' his writings may probably, displease many, we hope they will be agreeable to more, and that the people of this island will endeavour to examine candidly and impartially, what are the truths and falsehoods contained in the Letters of Battista Angeloni, tho' a Roman jesuit.

CONTENTS.

LETTER I.

TO the Reverend Father FRANCESCO MOLA, of the College of JESUITS at Rome.—Reasons why the Romans were ruined by a military force, and the English probably will not. Page 1

LETTER II.

To the same.—The liberty of thinking for themselves in matters of religion and government, as adopted by the Whigs, the ruin of liberty. 10

LETTER III.

To the same.—If the Whig principles were necessary at the time of James the second to preserve liberty, those of the Tories equally so at this time. 20

LETTER IV.

To the Reverend Father PAOLO SEGNERI, at Rome.—The causes of suicide in the old Romans and modern Britons assigned. 27

LETTER V.

To the Reverend Father ANGELO BONCARO, at Rome.—Whether the Italians are not as happy in their enthusiasm for religion, as the English in theirs for money. 42

LET-

CONTENTS.

LETTER VI.
To the Reverend Father STEFANO LORENZINI, at Rome.—*Comparisons between the external objects of Rome and London.* p. 50

LETTER VII.
To the Reverend Father DOMINICO MANZONI, at Rome.—*On the little regard paid to literature in London.* 59

LETTER VIII.
To the Reverend Father FILIPPO BONINI, at Rome.—*Praise of the ministry in promoting the propagation of the king's subjects.* 67

LETTER IX.
To the Reverend Father DOMINICO MANZONI, at Rome.—*A philosophical examination of national religion.* 71

LETTER X.
To the Reverend Father ANTONIO COCCHI, at Rome.—*Presbyterians and Papists equally avowers of infallibility.* 79

LETTER XI.
To the Reverend Father FILIPPO LAURA, at Rome.—*Not luxury that ruins a state, nor parcimony that saves it, instanced in France and Holland.* 85

LETTER XII.
To the Reverend Father DOMINICO MANZONI, at Rome.—*The effects on a nation, by insuring houses, ships, &c.* 97

LET-

CONTENTS.

LETTER XIII.

To the Reverend Father LORENZO FRANCIOSINI, at Rome.—*Whether the ridicule is not equally strong against the English, for suffering public companies to eat them up, as against the Italians for permitting Monks.* p. 105

LETTER XIV.

To the Reverend Father CURTIO MARINELLI, at Rome.—*England and France compared in their manner of conducting the two different kingdoms.* 112

LETTER XV.

To the Reverend Father FRANCESCO SANSOVINO, at Rome.—*The description of an odd character.* 121

LETTER XVI.

To the Reverend Father DOMINICO MANZONI, at Rome.—*The Quakers politically and religiously considered.* 128

LETER XXVII.

To the Reverend Father ANTONIO COCCHI, at Rome.—*The little knowledge in the ministry, in applying enthusiasm to national advantage.* 138

LETTER XVIII.

To the Reverend Father ALESSANDRO ADIMARI, at Rome.—*Liberty not the cause of genius in a nation.* 145

LETTER XIX.

To the Countess of **** at Rome.—*English gallantry compared with the Italian and French.* 158

LET-

CONTENTS.

LETTER XX.
To the Marchioness of **** *at Rome.—English indelicacy in the married people.* p. 164

LETTER XXI.
To the Reverend Father BATISTA GUARINI, *at Rome.—The shell philosophy, and philosophers, considered.* 171

LETTER XXII.
To the Reverend Father FABIO MARETTI, *at Rome.—The reception of Italian fiddlers, and Englishmen of letters.* 183

LETTER XXIII.
To the Reverend Father ANTONIO COCCHI, *at Rome.—The ridicule equally striking in the English believing impossible stories, as in the Italians believing in saints.* 190

LETTER XXIV.
To the Reverend Father DOMINICO MANZONI, *at Rome.—The impossibility of governing a nation without religion.* 198

LETTER XXV.
To the Reverend Father ANGELO BONCARO, *at Rome.—The effects of Fatality received as a truth, by the individuals of a nation.* 208

LETTER XXVI.
To the Countess of **** *at Rome.—The cleanliness internally and externally of English and French women, compared.* 219

LETTER I.

To the Reverend Father FRANCESCO MOLA, *of the College of* JESUITS *at* Rome.

Dear Sir,

O compliment, however well turned in its expression or elegant in its conception, can impart a more flattering idea to an Englishman than that of comparing him with an old Roman; the valour, prudence, love of liberty and his country, with those other eminent qualities of our illustrious predecessors, are the attributes which he receives with most delight.

IF a foreigner, in company with a member of parliament who had that day sold himself and his country to the inclinations of a pernicious minister, nifter, fhould compare the fenate of Rome to the houfe of commons of Great Britain, he would fee a fenfible joy fpreading over his face, a civility in his actions and expreffions, forgetting for one moment that he had revolted from the virtue of his anceftors and committed the moft opprobrious action belonging to man.

There was perhaps a time when thefe iflanders might with much juftice affume the likenefs of thofe Romans who lived in the moft flourifhing and virtuous moments of the Roman ftate. When integrity was the greateft honor, poverty no fhame, and the fervice of their country their higheft ambition and deem'd their moft exalted virtue; but they are greatly deceived if they imagine the prefent race refembles the former.

Believe me, Sir, the miftake lies only in the point of time? If you advance more forward in the dates of the Roman empire, the refemblance is extremely remarkable; that venality which once raged in Rome reigns here with equal diftinction at prefent, and when I leave London, I fhall pronounce with as much truth

as

LETTER I.

as Jugurtha did at leaving Rome, *urbem venalem et mature perituram si emptorem invenerit.*

IF one may be allowed to judge of the different periods of the moral character of a nation and compare them with another whose race has been ran thro' all the various stages of the course, the Romans in the time of Sylla were like the English of this present hour, in the corruption of their hearts and their disposition to venal influence, and the ruin of this government is near the same date proceeding from the same cause.

NOT that I mean to shew or imagine that things will proceed or terminate in this kingdom exactly as they did at Rome, tho' the constitution is totally perverting from its original plan.

THINGS are not enough alike in nature, especially those which are compounded of such numerous parts as those that form a goverment, to permit a parallel between the progressive states of any two constitutions, one of which is already ruined and the other advancing a great pace; and yet there is analogy enough to predict the de-

LETTER I.

destruction of a present government by manners prevailing in it similar to those which ruined a former state.

From this it is, that the antiministerial part of this kingdom keeping in idea the progression of the Roman state too closely parallel to the English, and forming no certain judgment from the principles and manners now actuating and existing, conclude, that because a prostitute venality was the ruin of Rome and a standing army the executive power, that England must be ruined by a standing army also, and that as Rome fell under the subjection of one arbitrary man, the fate of this kingdom will terminate in like manner.

To me it appears, who see things, or, at least endeavour to see them, in a light which a native (generally too prejudiced) is less likely to behold them, that the standing army of England will scarcely be the instrument of changing the constitution of this kingdom, or a monarchical state the first alteration it receives.

In

LETTER I

In order to make an army oppress their fellow countrymen, it seems necessary that it should be much inured to conquest, detained long abroad in the kingdoms which they subdue, and exerting a despotism which the victor too often assumes over the conquered; by this new habit the temper of the whole soldiery becomes changed, thence indeed by an ambitious general it may be led to enslave the land of its nativity, absence having weaned them from that tenderness which they originally cherished for their native country, and a long exercise of power over those they vanquished totally eradicated the love of equality with those amongst whom they were born.

From this it seems to me it arose, that the Romans inured to conquest and power in the different parts of the world, under the command of Cæsar in Gaul and other generals in different parts, drowned all love for their country in the desire of power, and destroyed one another with as little remorse as they would a Gaul or an Asiatic.

How the Britons should come to this excess is not easy to conceive; they can scarce be led to conquest any where and long enough detained from home, to forget their native land by the exercise of power. Besides this, humanity towards the vanquished is every where at present ten times greater than it was in the days of Rome, and consequently an arbitrary disposition less obtained by residing in a conquered country than at that time.

ADDED to this, that unless the army be commanded by the king in person, or some one nearly related to him whose interest is inseparable from that of the reigning prince, there can not be much to fear; the general who has led the troops to conquest in a strange land will scarcely lead them to rebellion in their native soil; there generally subsists too good an understanding between the commander and potentate to form the least suggestion of his setting up a separate interest; and increasing his sovereign's power would probably lose his own. Tho' the soldiers are induced to love the prince under whose reign they conquer notwithstanding

LETTER I.

ing he never enters the field of battle, as well as the general by whom they are led to it, connecting each in the cause, yet is there little to fear from that union. Queen Anne shared the glory of conquest and esteem with the Duke of Marlborough, and every old soldier joins them in his praises, and yet they would not have made her absolute. For these reasons it seems only necessary that the king or some one nearly related to him be not the commanding officer, and England has nothing to dread from a standing army, mixed as it is amongst it's own countrymen, and its officers generally from the best families.

In truth, Sir, to me there does not appear to be the least dread of the loss of liberty from the army of England; the interest of the exiled family is almost extirpated, no Englishmen will contend in their favour who can make head long enough to create a mortal antipathy in each party, which might terminate in the ruin of both, and absolute power: Competitors for kingdoms are comets which bring plague, pestilence and slavery to the natives, let which side will prevail; and tho' this nation has been most

amazingly

amazingly refcued from tyranny by the indolence and inactivity of Richard Cromwell, who with the spirit of a man might have been absolute as his father; and by the timidity, want of munificence and change of religion in James the second; yet the same confequences are by no means to be expected always. A contefted kingdom renders the conqueror abfolute in general, and the vanquishing and vanquished party are alike flaves in the fecond generation. For this reafon if there was no other, I think that a revolution should never be attempted but to prevent tyranny, for tho' this favourite people has preferved its liberty by revolutions, yet if a calculation could have been made à priori of the probabilities, whether liberty would have been increafed or not by thofe tranfactions, it would have appeared ten to one againft that which happened in the end? Where then was their wifdom? and what reafon have they to expect, this fuperior favour of heaven above other nations will always attend them? Is it worth while then for two parties to contend when each muft fuffer fooner or later by the conteft? or are two men tho' both kings worth all the bloodshed of a civil war, when nothing is to be expected

by

by the change which may improve the condition of the inhabitants? Indeed the people of England are not at present in that taste of thinking, and yet perhaps their liberty in more danger of ruin than at any other time. It appears to me that mankind in most nations are so much civilized, that were not absolute monarchies already so firmly established, it would be extremely difficult to induce one part of a nation to inslave the other, by arms; tho' there remain innumerable other ways by which it may be done, one of which I shall endeavour to shew you in my next letter, and which I suppose will prove the prevailing power and destroying angel of this land. I am,

Your most obedient servant,

LETTER II.

LETTER II. *To the same.*

Dear Sir,

IT is not at all surprizing that you who judge of the manners of this nation from what has been written of them only, should form your opinion of its character different from that which really exists at this hour.

What you say with respect to the English in the time of Charles the first is true; but the two interests which inflamed the minds of this people into such extravagant enthusiasm are quite at an end, at least as to martial matters, neither the Lord of hosts nor the king has one soldier who will fight his battles independent of his own private interest, tho' perhaps each party exerts as much prating in their favour as at any time whatever.

What I mean is, that neither religion nor the preservation of a crown in the same family, will make the people cut one another's throats, in this island, at least in this part of it.

To whatever excess the Tories have carried the notion of indefeasable hereditary right and
non-

LETTER II.

non-resistance, how much soever the idea of a king is to be considered as sacred in their principles, the prevailing opinion of the Whigs running into the opposite extreme and considering the crowned head as the servant of the people, hath as much destroyed the true constitution by that means, as it would have been by the former had it been carried into execution.

Men will speculatively support an opinion with vehemence, the ill effect of which they do not feel, which opinion carried into practice, those very identical persons will oppose with all their might; and therefore those very Tories who preached so much in favour of their passive doctrine, would not have acquiesced in the sufferings of an arbitrary power, and thus probably the due poise of the government might have been adjusted.

Whereas the Whigs spinning the web of their system too fine for the turbulent nature of mankind and more subtle than any government is capable of being well directed by, giving the king his power, the people its liberty, on such nice and exact distinctions, ideal only, at least

with

with respect to long duration, have by pretending to preserve their privileges usurped a right which by no means belongs to them, and placed the sovereign in a situation infinitely below his true degree.

Nothing appears more exquisitely combined to an unexperienced examination than the English goverment, where the executive and legiſlative powers, controul each other so perfectly, where the prerogative of the crown and rights of the people are so nicely adjusted and counterpoised; it is indeed a fine machine in idea, yet the fabric is too delicately wrought to go long well, and subtilty of workmanship wants strength of parts to sustain it.

In real truth the oligarchic government has been gaining ground ever since the revolution; the reason of it seems to be this.

At the time of king William's being fixt on the throne of Great Britain those who placed him there were the Whigs, who, tho' they might pretend an attachment to his interest, had really no other inclination than an increase of their own

LETTER II.

own power, difguifed under the pretence of preferving liberty, and which at that very time was really true in its effects, tho' not in their defign.

But as it was the ftanding and avowed principle of thofe men in power to affert that every man had a right to think and decide for himfelf in religious matters, to deride the clergy and inveigh againft their tyrannic difpofition, it naturally became impoffible to reftrain thofe perfons from thinking for themfelves in all affairs civil as well as religious; thofe who have indulged themfelves in every kind of latitude in examining the objects of religion and infift on their right to it, will never ftop from that of government; if they have a right to act with freedom in one they will alike purfue it in the other, the minds of men are not capable of fuch nice feparations, if they are indulged in one they will ufurp it in the other, and the confequence will be that if they conceive they have a right to decide for themfelves in matters of religion and act in confequence of it, fo in thofe of government they will apprehend they have an equal right, and will endeavour to act in confequence of that alfo.

Thus

LETTER II.

Thus the love of power being so natural to man, it has followed that the miniſtry of England have gained in arbitrarineſs ſince that time, and the kings and the people loſt their rights.

The Whig miniſter then from the nature of man and his own principles, which are built on ſelf intereſt, muſt be ever increaſing his own power and infringing thoſe of his maſter and the liberty of his ſubjects: as it is the love of power which generally leads men to the adminiſtration of a nation, ſo that ſame deſire of ſuperior influence exerts every art to increaſe it, and continue them in that ſituation; and in fact the Whigs have put in practice every artifice that can diminiſh the royal prerogative, the people's privileges and liberties, and are at laſt become a kind of traitors to both, and not much different from uſurpers.

They have all along conſidered their maſters as neceſſary to offer to the popular eye, to ſcreen themſelves, and to remove the ignominy which would have too apparently fallen upon them in many inſtances; and the people as a

bugbear

LETTER II.

hugbear to be offered to their princes fears, mixed with the word Jacobite, whenever they intended to quell any rising obstinacy in their breasts.

Added to this, they have duped the nation to their interest by an enormous debt and public companies of banks, South Seas, and East Indies, by which proceedings the monied part necessarily becomes so deeply interested in the preservation of this kind of administration, that a minister is here an absolute power.

Not content with this degree of certainty in preserving despotism, it has been the universal practice to spread venality through every little borough in the kingdom; by this may not every man be returned member of ———— who is furnished with most money from the treasury? and may not the senators of Britain in future times be no longer representatives of a free people, but the representatives of the ministers inclinations? from this source may not some future more corrupted man become so firmly fixt in the administration, that, far from fearing the being dismissed from his office, he may even threaten the *king* to leave his service (if one can

use

LETTER II.

use that last word on such an occasion) unless his demands are complied with?

Would not success in such a design be an absolute power? when the minister has nothing to apprehend from the prince's displeasure, and those who should be the trustees of the people's rights and immunities are all chosen by him, and each assigned to the borough he shall pretend to represent, and obedient to his will.

These last then are the standing troops which will destroy the constitution of Great Britain, and are more to be dreaded than the army, as every thing still bears the specious appearance of the ancient government. Here is the ———— and the ————— and who shall dare to suggest that every thing is not transacted by them void of all undue influence?

Every new way of destroying a government is much easier executed than one that has been already put in practice, the minds of men are alarmed by the similarity of the second to the first, and therefore are easily led to observe it; from this it happens that whilst the Whigs have been cry-

ing

LETTER II.

ing out against popery, passive obedience, and arbitrary power, the eyes of the people have been drawn to those objects, and never attended the silent path by which these exclaimers stole to power; in this imitating little thieves in a throng, one calls your attention to the right whilst another picks your pocket on the left. They thought they had once suffered from the two former causes, and therefore believed it probable they might again; but being never accustomed to, or indeed capable of investigating the true cause of any thing, or perceiving where the principles of the Whigs would terminate, lulled with the music of that song of liberty which was for ever chanted in their ears, that the king's power was diminished by the revolution, they conceived it impossible they could be enslaved from another quarter; and because they saw their prince's authority decline, they concluded it impossible that it could increase in any other place. This will finish the life of liberty in England, not unobserved by numbers, tho' too few to prevent its fall, nor unopposed by those who to the honor of themselves and fellow subjects would, have rescued their country from ruin, if true reason-

reasoning, or public utility, had any longer found attention in the nation.

PERHAPS, in using the term slavery, I have aggravated the condition of the English beyond that state in which it really at present ought to be considered, tho' I fear absolutely beyond recovery; every individual being disunited from the other, without any common principle to hold them together; open to venality, vending the public good for private interest, and regarding honor, patriotism and its attributes, as visionary ties of deluded and mistaken men.

PERHAPS, if the united kingdoms of Great Britain and Ireland were not so extensive, something like the Venetian government might one day be the fate of these kingdoms; but as they seem too large for the nature of that constitution, as the people have so long tasted of kingly government mixt with liberty, the sway which aristocracy or oligarchy would bear over the people would be too ungrateful, and drive them to the surrendering themselves entirely to the disposal of the prince upon the throne; and thus despotism in one, take its rise from the desire of avoiding

LETTER II.

avoiding the despotism of many, as it once happened in Denmark.

I presume you are tired with this long letter; I therefore give you my benediction, and dismiss you with the truest assurance, that I am,

Your most obedient servant.

LETTER III. To the same.

Dear Sir,

YOUR compliment, in answer to my last, merits my best acknowledgments: you desire me to give you my sentiments, on what would have been the fate of England, if the Tories had continued in the administration; but this is an affair composed of such different and entangled parts, that it will be almost impossible to develope what would have been the consequence; it will be more difficultly decided, than the famous question in Livy, where that author examines, what would have been the success of Alexander's arms, if he had turned them against the Italians, instead of the Persians.

IF we consider a Tory simply, without connecting with it what all the Whigs never fail of bestowing him, in my opinion, he is the properest minister; a man of his principles must conceive the religion of his country, the prerogative of the crown, the rights of the people, something above himself; as he acknowledges he has no right to think different from the esta-

blishment

LETTER III.

blishment in either case. Whereas, every Whig must imagine himself above all these; because he imagines he has a right to think, and determine for himself in each particular. And certainly it is the nature of that man, who thinks he has a privilege of accepting or refusing whatever parts he pleases in any government, to be less bound by it, than those who look on the three above mentioned articles as sacred. The constitution is for ever unstable from principle, in the hands of a Whig, and fixt in that of a Tory: For tho' this kingdom received its ultimate degree of perfection, at the accession of king William to the throne; yet that principle of changing, which has insensibly prevailed since, has totally destroyed the true state of the government then established, in every thing but nominals; after that change, it was absolutely necessary to be steady.

Supposing that the catholic religion, and the return of the Stuarts, would have been the necessary attendants of a Tory ministry; things which are always connected in the idea of a Tory by a Whig; it must be difficult to ascertain, what would have followed such a change, or how far

LETTER III.

far the mistaken zeal of those catholics, whose fiery imaginations pushed king James the second into such precipitate discoveries of his religious faith, would have carried them?

YET, give me leave to assert, that, if the Whig principle was necessary to preserve the English in their freedom and religion, at the revolution; the Tory is equally necessary at this moment, unless they prefer no king and no religion, and madly imagine a nation can be well directed, without either of them, and their constitution preserved.

WHATEVER was the opinion and design of the Tories at the revolution, however fixt their attachment to the Stuart race might be, at that time, those notions at present are at an end; they now defend the royal house on the throne, with as much zeal as the Whigs, and can only preserve the kingdom from the anarchic state which threatens it, before it totally takes its last unalterable change. In fact, unless the Tories have the administration, or their principles are adopted, the English constitution is at an end: it is become as absolutely requisite to oppose the oligarchic power at present, as ever it was the monarchic, in the time of king James the second; and the principles of the Tories will soon be as necessary to defend his present majesty, and the people's rights, from the usurpation of the ministry, as those of the Whigs were in the reign of king James the second, to protect the people's liberties alone.

NOTHING is so apt to deceive mankind, as specious plans of government, ideally delineated on paper: what can be finer imagined than this of England? but it is in this instance, as in the most highly finished machines; a dust stops their motion, or produces an irregularity. If men were all reasonable beings, and their whole drift and design were to render each other happy; if no intervening passions would interfere, to disturb the regular disposition of things, and the principles of a government once established would proceed as uniformly as those in mechanics; the Whig plan of the English constitution would be the best adapted for human nature, and human happiness.

BUT alas! such is the temper of man, that something more material and hardy must make

LETTER III.

up the component parts of a government, than those which are imagined in the whig syftem.

If a king fuppofes that he has an indefeafable right, and his minifter indulges him in that imagination; a militia, which was the ancient military force of this kingdom, and the gentry which command it, will never bend to fuch a difpofition, carried beyond what the laws allow.

No king has an indefeafable right to more than what the conftitution allows him; and this is, and may be fafely granted: whatever more the fpeculative zeal of a people may yield him, their fenfations will contradict and correct; and real feelings banifh the influence of ideal notions. Thus, in this very manner of confidering things, the king's defire of power muft be oppofed by the people's love of liberty; two objects of the fame ftrong paffion, which, meeting like the fides of an arch in the central ftone, fupport all firm and connected.

If a ftranger may judge of a nation he has long lived in, the prefent natives are miftaken

in

in what is every day advanced in public places, that the Tories are become Whigs, and the Whigs Tories; which is, that the minister has adopted the principles of the Tory, tho' he calls himself a Whig, and the Tory opposes on those of the Whigs.

But I think nothing has less truth in it than this assertion; the Tories have no inclination to oppose the king, they bend their force against the minister alone, whose power they see every year so enormously increasing; and the minister has no inclination to augment the regal prerogative, and only advances his own power: thus it appears that the Whigs are still Whigs, tho' in power; and the Tories still the same, tho' out of it.

This is the true state as it appears to me, and the Whigs are conscious of it; for which reason they brand with the opprobrious term of Jacobitism, all those who are in the opposition to their measures. And as the million judges from words alone, without distinguishing ideas, this keeps their schemes from being examined, and their opponents doomed to a kind of infamy.

ME.

LETTER III.

METHINKS I have given you an account sufficient to let you into the present situation of English liberty; I have no more to add on this subject, and only desire that you would conceal these Letters, which I may from time to time write you; perhaps there may be greater freedom in them, than the nature of our order allows, or at least, than some warm heads will permit, who cannot bear a difference of sentiment in matters of this nature. Adieu, I am

Yours most sincerely.

LETTER IV.

To the Rev^d. Father PAOLO SIGNERI at Rome.

Dear Sir,

IT has been my frequent obfervation, that when man cannot account for any phænomenon which is characteriftic of the manners of a nation, they immediately feek affiftance from external nature, to explain the appearance and effects of internal. Indeed, a late writer of great merit would folve all the difference of governments on the face of the earth, by referring them to the variety of air, climates and foils, which are to be found upon it; and thus, by placing words in the ftead of ideas, foothe us into a folution of that phænomenon, which he yet leaves unaccounted for.

It is ten thoufand times eafier to fay, that the air, climate, and foil of Venice, have been the caufes of the government which exifts in that city, than to trace the thoufand intricacies, which lead back to its real fource.

LETTER IV.

To me it appears, that nothing which affects the body in the manner which those external objects must affect it, can be the motives to any considerable changes in government; they may make men more or less healthy, fatter or leaner, hotter or colder. But as all parts of government take their rise from the powers of the mind and casual circumstances in its progression; methinks, to that all changes and constitutions of it should be refer'd.

Would it not puzzle a philosopher who espouses this airial system of government, to assign by what wind the little republics of Lucca and St. Marino were blown into Italy, surrounded with dominions of another kind; and preserved during the change of the rest? Or whence it arises, that the very city which you inhabit should have felt such remarkable alterations? Are the climes and all material objects so totally changed since the days of Cincinnatus, that the revolutions of Rome can be deduced from those causes? Have the winds of liberty forgotten to blow over that city, and the soil refused to lend nurture to its seeds?

That

LETTER IV.

THAT the effects of climates and exterior causes operate little in producing the various forms, by which mankind is governed, methinks we need to seek no other proof, than that sameness of government which prevails thro' the continent of America, where (according to the accounts from the best travellers I have conversed with in this kingdom, who have often visited the various nations which inhabit that part of the earth, and resided long with them) they are all held by one kind of constitution, from the least habitable parts of the north, to those of the gulf of Florida; and even the more southern division of Mexico and Peru, tho' the Spanish writers have given such formidable accounts of their emperors and incas, have no remaining traces which can lead a traveller to believe their stories; this renders their accounts to be suspected, and that the vanity of being deem'd conquerors of great nations, may have supplied their imaginations with what was deficient in reality.

IF winds, soil, and climates, were the efficient causes of that great variety of forms in government, which subsist on the face of the old world; it would be reasonable to expect the same consequences

LETTER IV.

sequences in the new, where these causes have equally operated, and America should therefore teem with all that is to be found in Europe in that kind.

Yet, Sir, if we disclaim all resource from these causes, do not we deliver up the vessel of philosophy to the direction of winds and waves; and losing that which may pass for a reasonable account, tho' without foundation, set our minds into disquietude, and thus become more unhappy by this discovery, which tends to tell us we have been deluded.

Shall we then say, that suicide amongst the ancient Romans and present Britons, is owing to the winds, air and soil? If we should pay this complaisance to that opinion, how will it help us to explain, why Rome has lost that iniquity, and England found it? Why it deserted that land, where it is no more known, and fled to this, where it never found admittance in former times? or shall we risque the assigning some cause, which may explain this phænomenon. Notwithstanding this custom of self-murder has so greatly prevail'd in each nation, I am far from thinking, that it took its rise from the same causes in Rome,

and

and in England; the education of Roman youth was military, and a contempt of life was of consequence inculcated into their first ideas, and grew up into a total possession of their souls.

BESIDES this, the nature of their religion does not seem to offer such reasons for the fear of death, as the Christian; nor is it yet quite evident to me, that the Romans believed in a future state: if Tully in some places seems to give countenance to such a belief, in others he contradicts it; and Tacitus, and he, I think, ascribe the intrepid behaviour of the Germans, to their expectation of rewards in another world, for dying gloriously in this.

DOES not this seem to intimate, that the Romans entertain'd no notions of future existence; at least, that it was not the popular opinion, or even the philosophical? and if they expected no reward it is scarce probable they feared punishment.

THUS it seems that their disposition of killing themselves arose from a contempt of life, early ingrafted in their minds, not conceiving it worthy the dignity of a Roman to live in misery,

LETTER IV.

fery or dishonour, either ideal or absolute, for the sake of preserving that simple property, existence.

FROM this resolution their religion could not terrify them; it did not tell them, that the sufferings of this world lead to the felicities of a better; or that the crime of self-murder would be attended with punishment hereafter: they had nothing to hope by tarrying here in affliction, and nothing to dread by leaving it, thro' their own voluntary inclinations; and thus the love of life alone was not sufficiently prevalent to withhold their hands from suicide, unassisted by the two prevailing passions of hope and fear.

IF you should have the goodness to indulge me in this account of the cause of the Roman suicide, it will serve me but little, I fear, in this of the English. These men are Christians, I think I may say it to you, who see things with the least prejudice of all men, tho' our faith scarce allows it to them; and yet I believe we must have recource to the reformation and its consequences, for the cause of this unnatural practice. In endeavouring to trace this to its source, we may perperhaps find the reason, why it no longer prevails in Italy; and discover the cause of its prevailing

in

LETTER IV.

in this kingdom, to be owing to the neglect of that which is observed in catholic countries.

'Ever since my residing in this nation, when I have heard of this rash act of self-murder being committed, and have endeavour'd at the knowledge of the character of those persons who have been guilty of it; it has constantly appeared to be from poverty, from which they saw no way of relieving themselves; from a religious melancholy, where the fear of future punishments has weighed down thir souls so heavily, that they have fled from this insupportable burthen, to the very place they dreaded, the present pang was too dreadful to suffer a moment's delay; from disappointment in their desires; from having amassed large sums by the most iniquitous means, inattentive in the sultry day of youth and action, to the horrors which must succeed in the chilly evening of old age; or lastly from having been equally abandoned thro' the love of inordinate pleasures in their youth, and stored their breasts with seeds of tortures for the inquisitive hour of conscience; one or other of these has been the visible cause of their suicide.

LETTER IV.

No man is so partial to his own religion, to imagine that the catholics have not seeds of the same dispositions in them; whoever is accustomed to confess those people, will find them there; but then they possess a cure which the protestants have not, and can fly to the salutary and soothing expedient of a confessor, where the mind disburthens itself in secrecy and safety, and comes back lighten'd from its woes, like a galley-slave from his fetters just knocked off. Every person who has felt affliction, or observed the consequences of it in others, must have perceived how greedily that condition of the heart pours out the story of its sufferings and calamities. So earnest is it of seeking some ear to whom it may unfold its state, that the desire of obtaining present ease very frequently urges men to discoveries of what they ought to conceal, and to persons who they are convinced are no friends, and whom they ought not to trust.

In many instances they dare not put this into execution; a confession of former iniquities would be certain death, irreparable disgrace, or total ruin: thus the mind continues harrassed, till it flies to that, which is the greatest of all terrors, to avoid the present.

THOSE

LETTER IV.

Those in that situation have no relief in the religion of England. To whom shall they confess? Who can be safely trusted with the important secrets of life, reputation and property, that will not reveal them? Whereas in the catholic religion the confessor hears this, and no dread of discovery haunts the mind, which has opened its whole cabinet of secrets; he sooths the afflicted into some contentment of their state, and alleviates their misery. It is to the want of this resource in England, that this horrid crime of suicide is chiefly to be attributed, and to the power of confessing the most atrocious actions, that it prevails no where in catholic countries.

Pray tell me, Sir, you who have been long inured to the secret recesses of human hearts, and found consolation for thousands in distress, whether this which I have been saying, may not offer some reason for the common practice of self-destruction so frequent in England, and its deserting our country? During my residence here, I have never known one catholic who has been guilty of it.

To me it appears that the reformers of the English church were extremely mistaken in abolishing

LETTER IV.

lifhing auricular confeffion. To diveft the prieft of the power of the peoples confciences they gave them into their own hands, who are very bad keepers of them; and thro' fear of being held in flavery, as they call it, by the church, they refigned themfelves up to be actuated by that evil principle which reigns more or lefs in every breaft; which Xenophon has finely defcribed in his Cyropædia, in the ftory of Panthæa, to have actuated Arafpes, and which the Chriftian religion calls the devil.

Is it not true that the minds of men require as much attention, to be preferved healthy, as their bodies? And tho' we pay the greateft regard to the latter, in chufing all we eat or drink, yet difeafes will arrive, and we are obliged to fly to fome fkill, fuperior to our own, or we run the rifque of being deftroyed.

Is it uncharitable to fuppofe, that health of body is more the concern of human nature, than fanity of foul? Or that it is lefs folicitous to preferve the latter from ftains, than the former from every thing which may defile it.

LETTER IV.

If it is not, it must require more relief, and more frequent application to the latter, than attention to the former; the mind of a man will no be more at ease under the thoughts of great crimes, than a beauty under that of a tetter creeping upon the rose in her cheeks, and spreading deformity; and yet in these mental diseases, there are no remedies provided in this land. Is not this to be ignorant of human nature, and a want of the greatest proof of political skill; that of keeping people easy in themselves?

Perhaps it is in part from this cause, that there is almost an universal restlessness in the behaviour of the people of England; they are steady in nothing but the love of wine, which dissipates their disquietude whilst they sit together; we see them moving from seat to seat in company, with every symptom of the *tædium vitæ* on their countenances and actions. In assemblies, without being present; riding and driving from one public place to another in search of new objects, which after a week become as dull and unentertaining as those of their own homes. For this reason you see more people on the roads of England

land than in all Europe, and more uneasy countenances than are to be found in the world besides.

One great excellence in the government of mankind, is to prevent as much as possible the inhabitants of a country from running into excessive disorders, which are fatal to the happiness of the people; and the most effectual way of obtaining this advantage is the coming to the knowledge of them the soonest possible.

The mind which has been tainted by its first crime, generally feels inexpressible compunction for that commission, and would gladly lay hold on the occasion of being reinstated in its former tranquillity. Yet, such is the nature of human frailty, it seldom has force enough to obtain this without assistance; the pain harrasses him that has lapsed, to drown it in company and excess; and that again pushes him to farther outrage; till at last time hardens that heart which before was sensible of its offence, and the delinquent goes on to destruction, or old age, when all recoils in horror on the sedentary and inactive soul.

This is frequently prevented by confessing the first error, the offender finds such lightenefs

LETTER IV.

of spirits after this discharge, such ease spreading over the soul, recalling peace and pleasure, like a flower drowned with excessive rains, or like the sleeping animal awakened by the genial sun-beams; that he dreads the relapsing into his former state, and is reclaimed entirely. The soul in the guilt of offence is careless of itself, it heedlessly lets all run to ruin, but when it becomes depurated by this act of confession and comfort; it takes heed to its paths, and enjoys the felicities which are allotted to human nature.

The human mind is like a pool, into which some filth will flow with the purest water, and requires cleaning at certain times, or the whole element becomes corrupted.

You must have observed, Sir, that a son who falls under the father's displeasure, if it continues, seldom amends his life from it, the pain of having offended, leaves him entirely restless and unheeding; he commits yet greater offence from that very uneasiness which was caused by his offending. Yet let a reconciliation be once obtained, he feels a pleasure and ease unknown before, and having freed himself from that anxious situation, sins no more, and lives in peace and felicity.

LETTER IV.

'To this want of easing the mind by confession, is to be attributed the frequent commission of suicide, tho' indeed many of these desperate actions may be assigned to the being awed by no god, and influenced by no religion; a state not uncommonly found amongst the highest and lowest ranks of people in this kingdom.

If you converse with the natives of this country on this subject, they will either tell you, that their church allows and approves of confession, or that this use gives the priest an absolute power over the lives and consciences of the confessing.

Indeed, the first is true; but then there lies no punishment against that priest who should reveal the secrets committed to his ear; and thus the penitent has no security: And the latter they are mistaken in, since no man need be afraid of them who cannot hurt him. All revelation of secrets, by catholic clergy, is inevitably punished by death. Pray tell me then, have not these reformers divested human nature of its greatest consolation, and by the imagination of preserving themselves free from the tyranny of the clergy, rendered themselves slaves to those feelings and conditions which are more or less inseparable from

LETTER IV.

from the state of a man, from which very fatal consequences are hourly arising? To me it seems, they might have preserved this custom, without being thought guilty of popery, that heinous sin to presbyterian purity. Burn this, and believe me, most assuredly,

Your most obedient.

LETTER V.

To the Reverend Father ANGELO BONCARO, at Rome.

Dear Sir,

IT has been frequently remarked, that the happiness of individuals does not depend on possessions, and that the labourer enjoys the delights of ease and sleep, with a pleasure unknown to those who live in continual inactivity: One day of relaxation from toil is tasted with rapture, by those limbs which are exercised in work all the other six; sleep is exstacy to fatigue, and plain food delicious to the hungry. Whilst all these are past over, unaffecting the hearts or senses of those who live in one continual research of that which fails them in the possession.

IN like manner every people forms the idea of felicity from what it perceives in itself: The English are not more confident, that this island from Tweed to the Lands-end, (Scotland is excepted) is the most inviting spot of the universe, than the Laplander, who freezes beneath the arctic

LETTER V.

tic circle, or the negro who burns upon the torrid sands of Guinea, are of the places of their nativity.

If this be a weakness, it is a beneficial one; it reconciles its inhabitants to the place of their residence, and peoples the globe in a thousand places, which must have been otherwise a desert.

Yet probably it is no weakness in the nature of man, but the absolute and real condition of being human creatures: the ideas we receive from external objects, and internal sensations, form and compose the actuality of the soul, and these naturally make the pleasures of our lives. Custom and education are the basis of our judgments; things are considered right or wrong, true or false, more as they refer to these two parts in us, than as they are in the real nature of things. Abstracted truths are the conceptions of very few understandings, whilst those of relative ones, are general to all minds: the beauty, happiness, understanding, of all nations are examined, as they relate to each individual, tho' imperceptably, and determined to be more or less excellent, as they tally with

the

the ideas which we have formed upon these subjects; self steals into all our examinations, and establishes our judgments relating to mankind.

If this be true, that custom and locality form our souls and its pleasures, it of consequence makes us dislike or condemn those which differ from us; and therefore, whilst an Englishman wonders how an Italian can live in a land of popery and slavery; the Italian admires at the English libertinism, and want of all religion and police; in those two views it appears, to those English eyes who are accustomed to see our worship in such excess, carried into idolatry and arbitrary power, according to English judgments; and to Italians their liberty is licentiousness.

METHINKS liberty is but another name for ease; where the mind is in tranquillity under the government where it lives, the inhabitants may be denominated free, at least they cannot be termed slaves, where the chains are not felt.

EVERY

LETTER V.

EVERY Englishman's notions of happiness is included in riches; for that reason, wherever they travel, they conclude all the world are more or less happy, as they are more or less wealthy. When they speak of the deserted towns of Italy, they talk of their inhabitants as the most miserable of people, because they are not rich; trade, commerce, and bustle, are their only and eternal notions of felicity: the quiet, sedentary and contented man, is conceived as unhappy, because he is not in constant activity; whereas I believe, that the pain in getting riches, is seldom balanced by the joys they bring with them.

IN truth, money is all that is zealously pursued in this nation; the inhabitants have placed the whole of human bliss, in the possessing it; not conceiving that the mind of man may draw consolation and exstatic joy from other objects, with more ease and certainty.

WHEN these people, on their travels, see a poor Italian pouring out the warm devotion of his soul, before the image of his patron saint,
they

they conclude him a fool, or a deluded bigot, because he can draw no advantage from this image, which is inanimate and void of power; and laugh at this as idolatry, not once conceiving that the rapture which fills the soul of this devotee, is as real and effectual joy to him and his conception at that time, as if the image was impowered with all the acts of creation: yet these very men shall approve of the person, who, in commerce, sweats thro' the day, and passes the night sleeplesly, or him who demeans himself to act the lowest character to an idol minister, in hopes of that gold, which each is frequently disappointed of; or, if they lay their hands upon it to take possession, feel every parting shilling going from their fingers, like vitality from their hearts.

THE idolatrous adorer of gold is frequently deceived, if not always, in one shape or another; the religious devotee never: if he does not receive the boon he asks, he always rises from his knees with more happiness, than he fell upon them; and, such is the fabric of the mind of man, finds ease in asking, tho' disappointed, and continues that devotion thro' a

whole

whole life of penury, happy in his religious disposition.

The miser can never find ease in disappointment, and tho' he possesses what he adores, to a man of his temper gold can afford no more of what the world generally admires, than the statue of the saint does to the religious: the miser dares not touch the sacred hoard, and the marble cannot give. Thus, in each instance, it is the belief only, that each object of their devotion has the power of bestowing, which communicates their happiness, and no real reception in any other manner from either of them.

If we place liberty in the room of happiness, and examine whether the being slaves to the passion of wealth, and goaded on to the obtaining it, is not as painful as that of being subjected to the religion and laws of monarchic states; taking into the consideration the effects of custom, education, and belief, shall we not find that those people are as free as the English, at least as easy, chearful, and contented? which tho' not the ideal liberty of a Britain, is the true one of human nature; in which, freedom and

and ease are the same things, and the power or the passion which domineers over us, is equally a tyrant, whether seated without on a throne, or inwardly in our hearts.

For my self, I truly say it, were it in my power to choose which of those passions I would possess; the love of God in penury, or the love of riches in possession as a miser, even for the joys of this world, were they to extend no farther; I would seize the first, and renounce the latter: every disappointment on earth, the devout mind converts by hope into rewards in heaven; and every disappointment to the adorer of gold, is real torture.

I am therefore satisfied, that devotion yields more joy to the natives of Italy, than wealth does to those of England; and that the poor of each nation have no kind of comparison in their happiness; those of London having lost all influence of religion, and almost forgotten that there is a God, at least in practice; whilst those of Rome draw constant happiness, from his eternal presence.

To

To the philosopher it remains to decide, which is the most reasonable way of passing life? not to the English wiseman, who trying every single object of the various faculties of man, by what he calls reason, which is wealth, in this instance, judges truly of none: but to that man who knows human nature, its variety and weakness, its passions, senses, and sensations, the fallibility of its judgment and partiality to particular customs, and what it must enjoy to be at ease; to him I fansy, the difference of happiness will not be so wide, as the English conceive it, between the possessor of the Romish religion, and English riches; if it should, I own myself mistaken, and recall my opinion; and yet believe me, such is the depravity of man, I am perswaded, that the catholic Italian would renounce his faith, and patron saint, sooner than the Englishman his money, with a view of finding happiness in the change. I am,

Your most obedient,

LETTER VI.

To the Reverend Father STEFANO LORENZINI *at* Rome,

Dear Sir,

PERHAPS it would be difficult to find two cities, which resemble each other so little, as that which you inhabit, and this from whence I write. At Rome tho' there are marks of present grandeur, yet the remains of the antient edifices impart an air of dejection, and decline, which naturally awakes the sigh; whilst all London increases in architecture and inhabitants, and conveys no other idea, but that of bustle and business.

WERE we to judge of what passes in the streets on all days but the Sunday, we must conclude that the idea of a God is unknown in this country; here are no monks in processions, richly clad, bearing crucifixes, and relicks; no host carrying to the sick, to sweeten the moment of the soul's departure; the temples are shut, and their God seems exiled from that place,
where

LETTER VI.

where he is more immediately supposed to dwell: not a priest in the streets to be seen, but just at the times of, before, or after dinner, strutting behind a rosey cheek and double chin, to or from some table of good chear. Even on their days of worship in their churches, there is ten thousand times more inattention to their duty, than to the price of stocks in change alley all the rest of the week; and the fervour of their devotion to obtain a seat in paradise is infinitely short of that of procuring one in parliament, purchasing a good bargain on the exchange, or trying to obtain a good place at court: they are as cool and unanimated in their acts of devotion, as they are warm and active in those of getting riches; and their temples, and exchanges, are accordingly constructed within for those different dispositions; every family having in their churches a snug pew, a kind of closet, where they all sit and sleep, or employ themselves in any thing but their duty to the highest: whereas, in their places of commercial rendezvous there are no seats, they would be useless there, the zeal of gain keeping them standing to their duty.

E 2 Ox

LETTER VI.

ON the contrary, the streets of Rome are filled with religious objects, priests, processions, crucifixes, the living and dying attending and attended; the churches, ready to receive the rising devotion of the inhabitants, stand with open doors to yield them a place of worship; all has the continual air of religious exercise.

IN London, religion seems to be periodical, like an ague, which returns only once in seven days, and then attacks the inhabitants with the cold fit only, which physicians reckon the most fatal; the burning never succeeds in this country.

IN fact, the whole business of London seems to be designed for the kingdom of this world; and that of Rome, for that of the other. If it be true, as the protestants pretend, that we have too much pomp and pageantry, in our way of worshipping the author of our religion; is it not equally true, that they have too little? Shall we then, one moment dropping all attachment to every particular sect of christians, examine as philosophers, whether these assertions are true or false; and considering man as he is,

endeavour

LETTER VI.

endeavour to decide something more permanent, than has hitherto been determined upon this subject.

It has been objected against the catholics, in favour of the protestants; that the former have deserted the primitive way of worship, and introduced ten thousand frivolous and idle ceremonies into their religion, which find no countenance in the gospel; this latter, I think, has been fairly obviated in the writings of our churchmen.

But methinks, the supposing that the primitive mode of worship, when Christianity was in its infancy, before any kingdom or government had received it, should always continue in that state, is just as sensible as to say, that because we are at first children, we should always continue so; or, that our Saviour being born in a place for the reception of cattle, ought to be worshipped by none but cow-herds, shepherds, and grooms.

Every institution, religious or civil, must have its birth, progress, maturity, and decline

perperhaps, equally with animal nature. Things and fyftems, animate or inanimate, are obnoxious to this deftiny; and if it were not contradicted in the facred fcriptures, I fhould be inclined to believe, that even the chriftian religion, may one day or other feel this fatal effect, and a new difpenfation recall mankind from the vices it is at prefent precipitated into; at leaft, it feems neceffary in this country of apoftacy from the truth.

As there is no mode of worfhip laid down in thofe writings, which have imparted to us the dictates of Chrift; we may reafonably fuggeft, that chriftianity, like the firft religion of nature, was defignedly left in this manner, that legiflators and potentates might adapt it to the different fyftems of government which they pleafed; and to the nature of thofe inhabitants, amongft whom it was promulged: there are many paffages in fcripture which would fupport fuch an opinion, at leaft which feem fo to do.

For this reafon, the nature of all mankind being much the fame, in the days of the firft

LETTER VI.

propagating the gospel; their exercises, arts, commerce, and employments, being extremely few, except in Greece and Italy; it was necessary that much time should be employed in acts of devotion: the mind must be agitated like the ocean to keep it sweet, and every part of it, the passions, senses, faith, imagination, and reason, find some object which may answer to each faculty, to make it happy and at ease.

Those who have conceived that the original simplicity, which made the characteristic of the first christians, was always to continue, have been extremely ignorant in the nature of man: it was necessary to oppose, at that time, that deluge of deifying the most infamous of men, who from being less than human under the title of emperors in this world, would be gods in the other, or the whole effect of religion had been destroyed. But when this rage was abolished, human nature must again take place; tho' floods have drowned the lands and swept away the harvest, yet it would be absurd to think it must never be fair weather: tho' the common process of nature, seems necessarily interrupted by those revelations from heaven for some

LETTER VI.

some time, yet the former manners will return; and thus the progression of Christianity from its primitive to its mature state, has been as natural to it, as the passing from infancy to manhood. For these reasons, have we not done right to catch the eye and ear, by objects of admiration and influence? must not the faith be kept alive, by objects adapted to the credulity of the human mind; which disposition actuates indefinitely in human nature, if not the whole species; something must inflame us by enthusiasm to acts of virtue, and damp us in the hour when the evil principle presides; and thus secure us from violence and misdeeds.

THE reason of that man who does not conceive things in this way, is extremely limited; he is either differently framed, or not acquainted with what passes in himself, or in the hearts of other men; he decides from too circumscribed a knowledge, and calls that truth and right reason, which is the glimmering of a weak capacity, and only serves, like the dim sepulchral lamp, to light him to disease and death.

LETTER VI.

AFTER having advanced thus far, it may be allowed, that some governments, and some people, may require less pompous application to every part of the understanding, than others; but certainly no civilized nation can be happily conducted, without something of this nature.

IF the idleness of the Italians requires the attention of many religious ceremonies to preserve them from ill actions, and keep their minds active; the English, a busy commercial state, may perhaps stand less in need of such great numbers as are seen in Italy; if the imputation of idolatry be thrown upon us, because we abound too much with ceremony; if tyranny over the minds of the people, be the sarcasm which falls on the Romish church; we may reply, that irreligion is the consequence of neglecting the first, and anarchy, confusion, and immorality in the people, from the too much indulgence in the other, in Great Britain.

IF it should be objected, that by means of all that pageantry of devotion which is seen at Rome, the spirit which should animate the
christian

christian evaporates, and leaves the soul steril in acts of charity; it may be justly replied, that in Britain there is not enough to make the mind active, in search of beneficence. Thus probably, it may seem that something may be mended in each city, relating to the form and spirit of religion; and that tho' England requires less ceremony at this time than Rome; yet considering human nature as it is, there is more morality to be expected from that people, which has some object operating on every part of the mind, by the warmth of hope encouraging, and the chill of fear restraining; than from that where the whole number of individuals has almost forgotten, that there is a power which superintends, and is superior to man.

PRAY receive the bearer of this, with that respect which he deserves; and conceal the contents from your right eye, if you read it with your left; in truth forget this and remember me. I am, &c.

LETTER VII.

To the Reverend Father DOMINICO MANZONI at Rome.

Dear Sir,

PERHAPS no nation has produced greater geniuses, than this from whence I write this letter, in many parts of literature and knowledge; their philosophers, poets, and mathematicians, are esteemed and studied every where; and a reputation of learning attributed to them, beyond the other kingdoms in Europe. It is besides this, the peculiar honor of the individuals, that their productions have been owing to the force of their own genius, unassisted and unencouraged by any thing from the throne; even to this hour, there is not a single pension given to any one, as the reward of literature, unless it be to that apostate *Bowyer* of our order, who having revolted from the religion he professed, and disengaged himself from all the vows he had made (a liberty Sir Thomas

More

LETTER VII.

More thought that no man could conscientiously dispense with) receives a pension of two hundred pounds a year as long as he shall continue to write the lives of the *Popes*; how long this will continue you will judge from the nature of the man, a very sterile sample of which he has already given to the public; you would be delighted with the artifices which he has made use of, to imprint a belief of his being in continual danger of death from the hands or machinations of our order; it would not be surprizing to me, if I saw him Archbishop of Canterbury: So greedily those sensible people swallow the improbable accounts he gives them, and believe that a man, who thinks himself bound by no oaths, because he has a mind to break them, and that change of sentiment dissolves all obligation, is yet candid enough to tell nothing but truth in the tales he recites to them; after this can they laugh at catholics who give credit to the miracles of saints, and be surprized at the populace being in devotion before their shrines?

LETTER VII.

FROM this neglect of learned men it is, that the present decline of literature is so great: The men of letters have nothing but that harpy, a bookseller, to give them bread; and is it possible that an author will for the sake of honour alone starve, whilst he is giving the last finishings of his productions by repeated revisals, for which he will not obtain one shilling better price? Can the *nonum prematur in annum* find entrance here?

IT is a scandal to the nation, since letters have given the kingdom its greatest reputation, that those who deserve well on that account, should be constantly haunted by that fiend necessity; and whilst they are labouring for the instruction, happiness, and entertainment of others, be deprived of all these themselves.

EVERY thing that does not come from the hands of a genius, is either disesteemed, or pretended so to be: like the late king of Prussia in his tall troops, this nation receives none, of the common standard. A genius will shew itself, it bursts spontaneous like flowers from the earth; it is a native of this clime, and therefore requires no

artificial

LETTER VII.

artificial heat to bring it to perfection: This is the common talk of all; and yet the naturalist will tell them, that very few flowers in this varying clime blow well, without being shelter'd from the sudden blights and frosts which are natural to it.

Their neighbours the French are of another sentiment; the academy of science furnishes twenty pensions to men of genius; and their other academies honours and favourable reception to their members alfo; scarce a writer of note who is not at his ease, remains unrewarded. The celebrated Marivaux and Crebillion have been each very lately remunerated by the Marchioness of ——, who does honour to the king that takes her to his arms, and effaces every reproach by the favour which she shews to learned men and artists. It should be declared high treason for a king of any nation to have a mistress, or be served by a domestic, that is not a native of that land they live in.

Sovereigns who feel less controul than their subjects, from all kinds of inclination, are more liable to pursue their desires than other men; and indeed, speaking humanly, they will

LETTER VII.

and must be allowed in it; but then their follies should be converted to as much use as possible; and what they give their favourites, should return to the people. The sun which robs the fields of their fragrance by exhalations, restores it again in dews and friendly showers, to the refreshing those flowers which it parched in the zenith of its heat, and does not suffer them to be wafted to other lands, and denied to those fields which first yielded them.

In this nation a man of sense has very little power of assisting himself, and improving, in polite company; there scarce remains a person of distinction who pays regard to men of letters; and the ladies, who have good natural capacities, have not yet imitated the French, in what would be more laudable than following the cut of a cap, or the dressing their hair, the presiding at their own assemblies: there men of letters might meet, converse, and learn purity of manners, elegance of conversation, and decency of raillery, from the respect which men naturally pay to the presence of a polite woman. It is the ill fate of this

LETTER VII.

this nation to borrow the follies of France; and the good fortune of the French to adopt the excellencies of this ifland: You will fuggeft then from this continual intercourfe, what judgment threatens this kingdom, and what a glorious revolution there will arrive at laft.

IF genius furnifhes a man with ideas, it is education which affords them their drefs; not that of fchools and colleges, where the defire of following the ancients in their very expreffions, as near as two languages will fuffer it, deftroys the originality of thinking, which fhould appear in all writings, and gives that the air of copy and plagiarifm, which the knowledge of the world would otherwife have rendered new and original.

FROM hence it is, that thofe men of ftudy who have written on familiar fubjects, have drawn the characters in their works with a mock exalted and ftiff out-line, like the drawings of Albert Durer; and thofe who have never ftudied the claffics, but written from what they call life, are
too

LETTER VII.

too low, finical, and familiar, without that alert and eafy grace which is to be feen in the paintings of Watteau. The firſt have defcribed mankind as it is feen in moſt moral authors; the good unallay'd with weakneſs, the bad unimproved with virtues: The other as it generally looks in nature unexalted by fuperior touches of genius and underſtanding, a uniform nothing in nature, like cyphers without a firſt figure to add value to the fum; an every moment's object totally improper for entertainment or ufe.

This feems to be the true reafon why ſtrangers complain, that the writers in this language are deficient in a certain grace and elegance, which are to be found amongſt the French and Italians, at the fame time applauding their ſtrength of conception and hardineſs of expreſſion; the feeds of genius ſhoot out ſtrong in this foil, but the pruner's hand is not fufficiently employed to make them bear the moſt exquiſite fruit to foreign palates. If the manners, and way of life, ſhould change to that which is known abroad; the women dictate

elegance

elegance to sense, and grace to behaviour, and genius once more revisit this island, we may yet see the other nations of Europe surpassed in all the parts of fine writing.

Adieu, recommend me to ———

I am your most obedient.

LETTER VIII.

To the Reverend Father FILIPPO BONINI, *at* Rome.

Dear Sir,

IN my letters to you, I have frequently hinted how deficient the police of this nation is in the knowledge of laws, which may prevent indecencies, outrages and theft, but to do all mankind justice; if the legislative capacity fails in this respect, it excells in another; and if the English are not much restrained from destroying themselves and others, they are greatly encouraged to increase their species by every incentive to propagation. The number of the inhabitants makes the riches of a kingdom: of consequence, the minister who encourages the propagation of mankind ought to be esteemed a true patriot, and lover of his country; and from all I have gathered from antiquity, none ever excelled the present of this isle, in that particular branch of enriching a land.

MARRIAGES in general take some time before they can be compleated: Custom has made a previous courtship necessary, of months or years; this is loss of time, loss of inhabitants, and loss of wealth. In this nation, where the spirit of calculation is so much cherished, where lives, hours and days are strictly brought to account; and every minute's idleness comes into the computation of loss and gain; where the sabbath is look'd upon with an evil eye, because it destroys one year's labour in seven; every delay comes into question, and is considered as a loss; for this reason all due encouragement is given to the increase of mankind, not by the old Roman law of the *Jus trium Liberorum*, but by an act against marriage, and by incentives to what is called simply fornication.

THRO' fear however, lest so beneficial a scheme might languish and decay, objects are exhibited to catch every sense, which may induce men to serve their country; every print-shop has its windows stuck full with indecent prints, to inflame desire thro' the eye, and singers in the streets charm your ears with lascivious songs, to waken you to the same employment,

LETTER VIII.

ployment, left you should forget to what purpose you were born; for men are apt to forget their duty in this instance particularly. This is to know mankind, to serve a country, and be a minister; but as the night comes on, and the eye can no longer be solicited by visible objects, there are innumerable women who walk the public streets, and prompt their fellow-creatures with the soothing words of *my dear*, like Philip's slave, remembering them that they are men, and enticing them to their duty, and the enriching their country: The comedies represented on their stages have an excellent tendency to this patriot design, and all seems full of this useful intent. In this part of governing then, it must be allowed that the protestant legislators excell the catholic; liberty is the word; and therefore the harlots of England have full freedom to seduce all whom they can, and augment their species; whilst ladies of this order at Rome are confined to one part of the city, shut up from the public good; thro' a mistaken notion that they seduce the unwary, and spread disease to the destruction of particular happiness between men and their wives.

LETTER VIII.

This popish invention, of restraining propagation, is abominable; it is directly a contradiction to the scriptures, which tell us to increase and multiply. And therefore I hope his holiness will issue a bull, which may abolish this restraint from the Roman ladies of pleasure; and as the protestants of England have adopted the Gregorian style, tho' it was of popish invention, that you will in return stick the postures of Aretine in every window, and not suffering obstinacy to oppose reason, because it is protestant, give the same indulgence at Rome, which is to be found in London. At my return I hope to find every thing of this kind, as it is here; your streets fill'd with harlots and libidinous singers, with full liberty to propagate our species by law and public encouragement, unfetter'd by matrimony. I am

Your most obedient.

LETTER IX.

To the Reverend Father DOMINICO MANZONI, *at* Rome.

Dear Sir,

THERE is but one way, as it appears to me, by which the religion of a country should be examined by the eye of a philosopher; which is, if it answers all those faculties in human nature, which will find objects for themselves, if the legislature does not take this provision on itself; that is, the senses, passions, faith, imagination and reason of man, ought to be exercised and influenced by the various parts of a religion, established in all countries, where men must be restrain'd by mental ties from evildoing, and stimulated to virtue by hopes of future considerations. If we consider the nature of man, and compute as well as we are able, the number of those who ought to be intrusted with the liberty of thinking for themselves, or drawing conclusions in things relating to their own interest; we shall conclude, I believe, that the people of England are not the most likely to consider

LETTER IX.

sider themselves strictly tied to the rules of religion and morality.

THE man who examines, whether an action should be transacted or not, which would increase his wealth, (tho' not strictly honest) hesitates less at injustice than one following implicitly the dictates of religion, which tell him it is iniquitous, and will ruin his future felicity.

DEBATING on matters of interest, like deliberating in love, is attended with conquest on the side of passion; the love of money and the love of the sexes, carry it from the soundest reasoning which finds no assistance from hopes and fears; honor in one case, and probity in another, are extremely apt to yield in all contests, where the head and heart are at variance; and human nature unassisted by the ordinances of religion, has not virtue sufficient to be honest.

FOR this reason there must be checks made to these propensities in mankind, for the senses, as well as the other parts of the understanding. In this great city, where commerce and the love of gain, occupy all mankind in one shape or another,

LETTER IX.

other, the mind, hurried in amassing wealth, is apt to forget the strict rules of probity, tho' a christian.

It is not ill-founded, to my manner of thinking, therefore in human nature, that the Host should be carried publicly to the departing soul; it may be of as much use to the living as the dying, and awake a sense of duty in those who see it in the streets, who are apt to be remiss without frequent admonitions; it may suspend the hand one moment from deeds of injustice, and by awakening the hopes and fears which would otherwise lye sleeping, preserve men from imposing, and being imposed upon.

Without entering into the arguments for and against transubstantiation; as an affair of this world, is it not better that all Christians should believe it than not? will it not affect the mind with more solemnity, if the God of our worship be believed to be present in this sacrament, than not? and would that test of Christianity be permitted to be so trifled with, as it is by the protestants who pretend to conform to the established

LETTER IX.

blished church of England, if the real presence was received as the doctrine of the established religion? For the mutual advantage then of human nature, if the belief of the actual presence is not absolutely necessary, it seems requisite that the sacrament should be considered as the most sacred of all obligations: and yet, the corrupted heart, or pernicious head of a certain bishop of this nation, has produced a book on the Eucharist, with design to annihilate all consideration of its being sacred, a mere health to the pious memory of Jesus Christ, King William, or Oliver Cromwell; as if men wanted to have the restraints, which keep the mind from running into contempt of religion and her ordinances, rendered less obligatory than they are.

FROM this it is, that the Presbyterians, who are obliged to take the Eucharist before they can possess any place under the crown; most solemnly in the face of heaven receive this sacrament, the proof and pledge of their conformity to the church of England, the most sacred of oaths, and then totally disregard it the next day, and all their future lives; considering

LETTER IX.

ing it in no light but as a convivial ceremony. Should a man who can trifle with these institutions, be intrusted with the public welfare? Can there be an expectation of honor, or probity, in that heart, which has been mean enough to yield to so base, and so infamous a practice? Yet, the bishop has been exalted to the most acceptable see in the kingdom, by the minister, for this performance, and others equally beneficial; and his praise is the subject of all those who stand in need of support for the practices of occasional conformity; he has done more mischief to the cause of religion, than all the deistical writers of the world, and sapp'd the foundation of those principles which actuate more strongly than reason, in producing happiness in man: It seems to me, that the rebel to the religion of his country, should not be better treated, than the rebel to his king; even here I shall venture to say, that tho' they both ought to be preserved, religion and the prince, that the religion of a country is of as much consequence to its welfare, as the sovereign who governs it; and the person who employs his head and hand to the destruction of the esta-

blished

blifhed worfhip of his native land, is but little likely to exert them in defence of his fovereign.

FROM what has been faid, does it not appear, that the catholics are more philofophical in believing, and fupporting the belief, of the real prefence, than the Proteftants who reject it?

METHINKS the word truth, tho' it has made fo much clamour in the world, has yet never been well underftood; the reafon is, that few people have yet defined what it is. Every thing which is the object of faith, and received by any mind, is always confidered as true; therefore, the manner in which all things are conceived, is the particular truth of each individual mind: but as this muft for ever make one eternal clafh in the belief, behaviour, and actions of mankind, there remains, that the objects of faith not being capable of receiving any demonftrative proof, the utility which accompanies any of them is the only truth they can poffefs. Truth in this fenfe being abfolutely unlike mathematical truths, where every part is perfectly underftood, and the whole refult fairly comprehended.

LETTER IX.

In this instance, it means nothing but right or fitting: Thus, rain is truth, in respect to its being right and fitting for the productions of the earth, without which no sustenance is to be expected. The whole vegetable and animal world were originally formed with reference to this fluid; and in like manner the mind was divided into various parts, to each of which there are proper objects adapted by the hands of nature.

Does it not appear like reason to say, that objects adapted to influence the faith and passions to good works are true; that is, right or fitting for human nature; tho' they cannot be proved to be logically, or mathematically true. In what sense are the laws of a nation to be considered but in this light? We acquiesce in the belief of their being true, because they are right and useful, without seeing the reason on which they are founded; and we ought alike to to receive the objects of our faith as true, because they are right and fitting to our welfare.

The public institution of a religion and its objects, are the truth of religion in every country,

try, from which no one has a greater right to differ, than he has from the eftablifhed laws; members of focieties having given up all right in both to think for themfelves, at leaft to act and fpeak in confequence of fuch thinking.

THUS then, each religion eftablifhed is the truth of that nation in which it exifts; yet, there are fome religions more, and fome lefs, adapted than others to the public utility, in particular parts; and in this refpect of the real prefence, it feems to me more philofophical and wife, to adopt than reject that belief. A nation will be more probably reftrained from acts of injuftice and rapine where it is received, than where it is not, which is all that feems neceffary to conftitute the truth of things of this kind.

REMEMBER of what confequence this letter is to me, let it be beheld by no eye but yours; indeed your own intereft fpeaks plain enough, that it be committed to the flames. I am,

Your moft obedient.

LETTER X.

To the Reverend Father ANTONIO COCCHI *at* Rome.

Dear Sir,

THERE is nothing which the Proteſtants endeavour to turn into ridicule with more pleaſure, than the infallibility of the Pope, particularly the diſſenters from the church of England; and yet there is nothing in which the laſt reſemble us ſo much, as in that particular.

INDEED they carry the idea much higher than we do; for whereas we catholics, knowing that infallibility muſt reſt ſome where, or which is the ſame thing, an implicit obedience to the dictates of ſome one council or head, have modeſtly given this to the head of the church; whilſt the diſſenters have in direct contradiction, made each a Pope of himſelf; that is, ſet himſelf up as an infallible judge in all ſpiritual matters.

To

LETTER X.

To me it seems, if there be an abſurdity in making one infallible head, there is yet a greater in making ten thouſand infallibilities; and there is even more modeſty and reaſon, in allowing that the perſon who has applied his whole ſtudies and talents to the diſcovering and adapting religious objects to the mind of man; than in every taylor who leaps from his ſhop-board, or cobler who ſallies from his ſtall, ſetting up for an infallible judge in matters which he cannot underſtand, both from the nature of the ſubject, and the degree of his capacity: In England therefore, every Preſbyterian is a Pope, and in Italy there is but one.

It is the avowed principle of the Diſſenters in this kingdom, that each man has a right to decide for himſelf in affairs of religion, which is the ſame thing as to ſay, that men have a right to determine wrong in theſe matters; or, that every thing is both right and wrong in this ſubject. If two men are of opinions, that are diametrically oppoſite to each other in every tenet; each of them it is ſaid, has a right to decide for himſelf; one then muſt be wrong, or nothing comes

LETTER X.

come under that denomination; and thus, in consequence this man has a right to decide wrong; or which is yet more absurd, as they assert, that whatever each decides with respect to himself is the truth; it follows, that what is wrong being the same as what is false; right and wrong, truth and falsehood, are one and the same thing; this is yet a more manifest absurdity, than the infallibility in the Pope. The contradictions between truth and falsehood, right and wrong, are not incurred in the supposing that infallible power in one man, which are manifestly the consequence, in allowing it the general right of all men; hence it seems, that the Presbyterians and Papists do not differ in the article of infallibility, but where it shall be placed; whether every tinker, taylor, and mechanic, shall possess this power, as the Dissenters conceive, or in the head of the church, as the Papists profess to allow it.

INDEED, the established religion of England observes a medium between these extremes, and without allowing infallibility in the head of their church, acknowledges, that he has an authority to rule and determine what is, and what is not, to be admitted into their worship. Thus then, this heinous sin of supposing an infallibility in the Pope, so laughed at and ridiculed by the sectaries in this country, is yet more glaringly absurd in their own tenets and doctrines.

It is a settled law, that whoever obtains a place in the hands of the government in this kingdom, must take the oaths of allegiance and supremacy; that is swear fealty to the king, and renounce the Pope as being the head of the church; or, which is the same thing, that the king is the head of his church: this excludes all catholics, who tho' they would willingly take that of allegiance to the king on the throne, have not yet dared to trifle with their consciences and abjure the Pope; if this is no proof of their prudence, it is of their integrity; and that they are yet bound by some principle, as this circumstance excludes them from all places and employments of honor and profit.

The Presbyterians on the contrary, without hesitation swear allegiance, and take the oath of supremacy, allowing the king to be head of his church; which last article is contrary to the

first

first principle in their Diffention; that each man has a right to think for himself in religious affairs, independant of all powers upon earth.

Thus the catholic is excluded and diftrufted, becaufe he has conscience, honor and probity; and the Prefbyterian cherifhed and promoted, becaufe he trifles with the moft facred obligation on earth openly, in direct violation of his avowed principles. Methinks this partial toleration is knowing little of mankind, and being but weak in the great affairs of adminiftration. In defence of this they alledge, that the Prefbyterian principle is ftrong in favour of liberty, and the catholic of arbitrary power. The catholic Cantons of Switzerland are as free as the Proteftant; the Prefbyterian principle is in nature defpotic, and in the days of Cromwell, was the occafion of more bloodshed and defpotifm, than all the attempts of catholics have produced in this nation: did it not end in the hands of that ufurper as arbitrarily, as it could have done in Charles I's? and would it not have continued in that manner, if his fucceffor had been equal to the tafk of governing?

Nay

LETTER X.

Nay thefe very Prefbyterians, thofe advocates for liberty of confcience, were they not equally defpotic during the grand rebellion with what they impute to catholics? they had no fooner paft the ocean and landed in America, than they ill-treated thofe who differed from them in religious fentiments; inflicting that perfecution on others, which they exclaimed againft, and fled from themfelves. Thus it appears, that extremes are all the fame; fire and froft deftroy vitality alike, and a rank Prefbyterian is at the bottom fomething worfe, than what they fo liberally impute to us of the Romifh communion. I am,

Your moft obedient,

LETTER XI.

To the Reverend Father FILIPPO
LAURA *at* Rome.

Dear Sir;

WHATEVER may have been the cauſe of the decline of the Roman ſtate; it is not luxury which has been the ruin of this. Men are too apt to attribute the cauſe of things to ſome viſible object, which accompanies or precedes any change, and neglecting to examine within, miſtake the ſhadow for the reality. That nations are generally ruin'd when luxury prevails, may be true; but it is from the ſame cauſe that luxury and ruin come together.

PEOPLE of every ſtate that is poor, and driven to frequent diſtreſs, have no objects which can tempt them to eternal diſſipation; the ruling paſſions in that land, are the love of their god, and the love of their country; the ſecondary, themſelves. The Swiſs amidſt the delights

LETTER XI.

lights of France, pines to death thro' pure love for his native mountains; and the Dutchman, worth a hundred thousand pounds, sighs for lands of gold and ophir. The only bond which can unite a whole nation are the two first, and the last is that quality which dissolves this power of attraction, whatever is the intervening cause in a state, that dissipates the spirit of patriotism, or banishes the influence of religion, at the same time it lets the mind loose to all kinds of depravity and destruction. However, Sir, when I say that the last passion is that which destroys a nation; I would not be understood to mean, that the love of ourselves becomes culpable but in the wrong application and excess of it.

If we cast our eyes upon two neighbouring nations, we may plainly perceive, that luxury does not ruin, nor parcimony in the individuals save a state.

France, tho' it has been long practised in the highest luxury, in a much more refined and excessive way than is to be seen in England, or perhaps ever was known in any nation of Europe, has yet increased in power, extent, riches and sci-

ence,

LETTER XI.

ence, since the introduction of that taste amongst them; and Holland has sunk into contempt and ruin amidst the greatest parcimony, and most excessive meanness of saving: Hence it is evident, that neither luxury destroys, nor frugality sustains a state; but some uniting principle, which combining all the individual particles, moves the whole together, and imparts a force to the center, of the greatest importance, when the mass is once put into motion; it is this which preserves the consequence of a people; whereas each particle being let loose, and disunited, the whole moves without effect or regard. From these depends the good or evil of a nation; 'the first is a bullet which, from its union, driven from a cannon acts with efficacy and import; the other small shot, which disunited, have no effect but upon small things.

THE love of money, whenever it takes possession of the heart, declares war against all human nature. As the object of trade is the possessing riches; the more that pursuit is encouraged, the more will this love of money prevail, till at last it becomes the sole motive to all actions.

The

LETTER XI.

The Dutch, infatuated by the love of riches, have supplied the French during the war with that powder and ball, which was to be the death and destruction of their own native troops the next day; and the highest ranks amongst them have sold themselves, their towns, and nation's interest, till it is become contemptible, to the French; and thus are undone without one spark of luxury having ever been lighted up amongst them.

THE French officer, lost in luxury at Paris, no sooner hears the drum beat to arms, but he flies to the field, and behaves becoming the bravest man; his own honor and his monarch's glory form the union, and create incentives which actuate the whole nation to this behaviour. The Dutchman sculks in his town, and, contracted into himself, plods how he may draw some personal advantage and preserve self in safety from the circumstances around him. Thus the first grows great with his country's greatness; and the latter, meanly conceiving he can create a particular advantage from that of his country, blinded by self-interest sees it sink, tho' he must fall with it at last.

Thus parcimony does not save, nor luxury destroy a nation; it is some other disposition, blended with either, which must save or destroy a state. Every exercise of the love of wealth is accompanied with the idea of self, in augmenting its own stores, and diminishing those of others; or, which comes to the same thing, that of being richer than every one else: this disunites every man from every other, creates a separate interest in the breast of each individual, and increases the passion of self-love, which it is the duty of every nation to discourage; it destroys the universal good by fostering the private; thus nations become poor, whilst the individuals gnaw their way thro' the vitals of their mother into immense riches, or, like young pelicans, live on their parent's blood. Parcimony in the inhabitants of a country is a virtue, if they save from themselves to serve the public; and, like the old Romans, empty their own coffers to fill those of the national treasury. This frugality arises from a different motive from that which robs its country to enrich itself. This last sort of men esteem their own nation preferable to no other,

but

but becaufe in time of diftrefs, they can enrich themfelves by its ruin. It is the moft amazing of all things, what fortunes were made by thofe men who during the late war joined with the minifter and their enemies, to plunder this kingdom by loans of money at treble intereft, and affifted in endeavouring to fink that fhip which fcarce finds power of fwimming at prefent, except the tamenefs with which this iniquity was permitted; thefe are the nation's friends, if we are to believe the Courtier and Whig.

The idea of luxury in England, is ill underftood; it does not deferve that name; it is profufion only, another fpecies of felf: All that is expended here, at leaft the greateft part of it, is on the individual poffeffor. That of the table is at taverns, where each of the company pays for himfelf: In France the notion of liberality accompanies expence; the men of that turn impart to their friends and acquaintance, that which an Englifhman beftows on himfelf alone; the ten guineas, which this latter at a tavern fwallows felfifhly down his own throat at

LETTER XL.

London, shall be communicated in Paris with gaiety and good humour to a company, who are entertained with politeness and ease; even noblemen of great estates and high places in this country, will meanly send a turtle, to be eaten at a tavern amongst their acquaintance, club their five guineas with the others, and scuffle off large plates to be sent to their ladies, who admire it extremely, but do not like that their good men should have that liberality which makes the genuine characteristic of nobility, and entertain their friends at home. They tremble at the fatigue, poor women! and pretend they cannot support such hurry; as if they were the cooks, obliged to dress it.

In France, luxury is combined with liberality; this keeps up the mind to its true spirit: In England, with avarice; which debases it to the last degree. It is the selfishness of the Dutchman, and not the pleasure of the Frenchman, that threatens the ruin of this country, if ruin is to come from either of them.

Luxury, in the manner in which it is used in France, has the same effect that parcimony had in ancient

ancient Rome. In rich states the national supplies are kept up by the consumption of those articles which form the luxury of a state ; and the liberality, with which it is given, preserves a true spirit of generosity in the mind of men.

In Rome, poor in its beginning, the national expence could be saved from the private alone; the œconomy of the individual was only able to supply the wants of the public, and the minds of the citizens were enobled by thus giving to the general good.

In England where all is self, their profusion as well as their parcimony, the mind is contracted and debased, and the nation declining from that cause. If the chevalier de St. George was not to the minister what the devil is to sinners, it had been ruin'd long since : The one keeps many a christian honest thro' fear, as the other has many a minister from taking too hasty strides, to the placing themselves in absolute power: since the last rebellion, the eldest son secreting himself, and the other being turn'd priest, the terrors from
that

LETTER XI.

that quarter are much alleviated, and ruin advances with larger steps.

It is not in the luxury of eating alone, that this selfishness prevails; their collections of paintings, and other fashionable studies, are all for themselves. In France and Italy, those curiosities are made to shew how much the master is obliged to those who think them worth their attention. In England, to tell you how much you ought to be obliged to the master that lets you see them; the difficulty is great which you must overcome to obtain a sight of their curiosities, and the master considers it worth ten shillings, which the servant receives, and oftentimes double that sum: by this means a domestic in many families has as good an employment as many at court; and as much money has been paid for the seeing many houses, as they have cost building.

Thus, it is not luxury which threatens this nation with ruin; it is that mean self-love which is mixed in all the actions of the present generation, that is to be dreaded only on this account: the money which is spent, is not in the liberal and

and noble manner of their anceftors; when public tables received men of wit and learning; as in the days of Charles the fecond, and queen Anne; but in the purchafe of boroughs, and in that company of fellows who are pimps to the ruin of their country: this contracts the nature of their fouls into that of traffickers; the firft minifter is only a larger broker than thofe on the exchange, and deals in more pernicious commodities.

THERE are ten thoufand things which may be inftanced, to fhew the contracted fpirit of this nation; no painter, however excellent, can fucceed amongft them, that is not engaged in painting pourtraits. Canaletti, whofe works they admired whilft he refided at Venice; at his coming to London, had not in a whole year the employment of three months. Watteau, whofe pictures are fold at fuch great prices at prefent, painted never a picture but two which he gave to Dr. Mead, during the time he refided here. At the fame time, Van Loo who came hither with the reputation of painting pourtraits very well, was obliged to keep three or four fubaltern

painters

LETTER XI.

painters for drapery and other parts, whose pictures nine out of ten, from hurry and other things, are not better than the first signs which hang in the streets; yet, every one trembled left his own sweet face should not be drawn by him. Self is the most delightful object which self can behold; from this spirit it is, that painters of the superior kind never find encouragement in this city, the connoisseurs of this nation will not give six-pence for the production of any man who paints in their own country, because others can have the same performance; it must be the selfish idea of having what no other man has, which makes the pleasure of the possessor, and not the true merit of the production.

This, tho' it extinguishes all advancement of the imitative arts in the sublimest part of them, is of great use to the dealers in pictures; it has converted many a footy old woman into a Rembrand's; Raphael's, Guido's, Carrache's, and Titian's, are to be found in every collection, undoubtedly belonging to these painters, because the godfathers who gave them these names are still alive, and can answer for their being originals.

An

LETTER XI.

An Englishman of no note, thinks he cannot make you a more acceptable present than his own picture; as he knows that the dearest thing on earth to himself, is himself, he fansies he makes you the most valuable donation, in giving you that other self; tho' the whole actions of his life have been without one instance of a good heart, or good understanding. Thus, in a thousand instances of expence, all terminates in self, and communicates a contracted and limited spirit; whereas, liberality added to expence, enlarges and exalts the mind; the one resembles that peculiar power of attraction which belongs to particular bodies, which drawing only to itself, dissolves and counter-acts the general union; the other, that power which, diffusing its influence every-where, holds together the universal frame of nature, which is liberal and productive of all the benefits we receive. Adieu, I am,

Yours most obediently.

LETTER XII.

To the Reverend Father DOMINICO
MANZONI, *at* Rome.

Dear Sir,

I have formerly said in my letters to you, that the cause of the decline of religion in England, was owing to that liberty which each man takes, in deciding for himself in these matters; from thence it happens, that tho' there may not be more than five hundred nominal sects, yet there are almost as many different opinions as there are various heads; and nothing in either of them in which all unite; from this it proceeds that the true fire of devotion is dissipated in dispute, and the fervour which attends our worship annihilated and unknown in this country.

Tho' this discord makes great part of the neglect of public worship, and disregard of the author of all, yet there are other reasons which conduce to this effect, which were formerly unknown or unobserved by me.

LETTER XII.

It is natural to the mind of man to be more ardent in obtaining its desires, than grateful in its returns for the receiving the completion of them; the cause of the inequality of these passions, seems to me to arise from this, that no one thing which we can possess, answers to that excellence of it, which we have entertained in idea; the mind therefore being greatly disappointed in possessing the enjoyment which it expected to receive, becomes cool in its returns of gratitude to the Being who bestowed it; and this, whether it be to the Giver of all, or to our fellow-creatures?

Whoever therefore is at ease, and in affluence, is neglectful of acknowledgments; whilst the person in expectation, and desire, is active and humble: the first will be less busied in devotion to the God who has given, than the latter who expects: the first will sooner think himself independant of all things and all beings, than he who finds in himself dependance, and want of many things, and much assistance; thus riches create irreligion.

LETTER XII.

IF this be true, that kind of policy which renders men most independant of their Maker, is most likely to extirpate religion, and with that generally all the valuable qualities of the heart disappear; we give to those in want because we have tasted of that bitter cup ourselves, or because we conceive we may naturally fall into that condition; the man surrounded with plenty and security who has not felt distress, is less likely to impart, than another who is not in that situation and has tasted of affliction; this is generally found to be a true observation. Methinks therefore, this dependance on a superior power, should not be annihilated, since charity and probity depend so much upon the believing that we are in a state of danger, and in the hands of something superior to man.

SECURITY destroys our fears and our devotion, and thence in great part proceeds this neglect of worship, which is to be seen in this nation; the power of insuring a ship at sea, or houses and effects at home, if what I have said be true, is therefore productive of this independance and neglect.

LETTER XII.

THE merchant who has secured his property by insurance, from waves, winds, and shipwreck, on the ocean; and from fires at home, is more at ease than if he had no such power of insuring; he is less apt from nature to ask protection from heaven, and be charitable with the view of receiving favours in return, than he who is under the actual influence of all these risques. Reason as you will on this subject, and exalt the notion of the human species as you please, such is the nature of man; he will less probably defraud, who fears being visited with calamities of the above kind, than he who, secure from these chances, pursues his interest, unadmonished and unchecked by such apprehensions. The insurers, on the other hand, where this loss of devotion in the merchant ought to be accumulated, compute and reason in another manner; they conclude from a computation of chances of all the ships which sail, and all the houses which are insured, and draw the idea of advantage and profit from the whole calculation; they are therefore unactuated from that spirit of devotion, by their security being diffused thro' the whole of commerce and building;

LETTER XII.

ing; their concern is too little in any one place to be much afraid for particular accidents.

Thus this idea of security in property diffipates the spirit of religion; the heart of him who is secure and at ease, is never so truly animated with gratitude, as his is with desire who wishes to succeed; and from thence this frigidity of devotion, and neglect of worship, is partly stolen upon this nation without their being acquainted with the motive.

Nothing is so flattering and prevalent in the minds of men, as the love of independancy; it is therefore no wonder that these insurances have so universally prevailed; yet, since no lucrative advantage to the whole community can be obtained by these institutions, the transfer of property only from one man to another, being the consequence of their loss or gain; it may be worth while for a legislator to consider, whether dependance in the mind of man on the supreme Being, should be lessened by these institutions, and the restraints from ill actions and incentives to good diminished, for the sake even of no temporal advantage to the whole.

LETTER XII.

IF the cause of God was simply to be opposed to the desire of wealth, I know this nation too well to doubt one moment which would be the victor.

IT seems to me also, that the great debauchery which is seen in this city, the total inattention to all acts of devotion, and irreligion amongst the lowest people, arise in great part from the same cause.

IN this kingdom there is an act of the legislature, which obliges all the parishes to maintain their poor; nothing seems more humane, or more worthy the care of a legislator, than this institution: scarce any man living, who had not seen the effects of this law, but would approve of it, and yet the consequence is this, that the streets of London are filled with such objects of misery, as are to be seen in no other city and no other nation.

THE poor claim the revenue arising from this tax as their proper right, they receive it without thankfulness, the giver does not bequeath it

LETTER XII.

it from the principle of charity, nor the receiver take it with the sensation of gratitude.

THE first depends upon it in sickness and old age, is less solicitous to save, than those of other nations, till he becomes habitually profuse; he sees the establishment is of man's ordaining, and not depending on charity, that principle established by providence in the human heart, is not touched with gratitude at the provision; whereas if this assistance came from the good disposition of the giver, the cause being invisible to vulgar minds, the God of all would receive their acknowledgment, and the spirit of devotion be preserved living amongst these most despicable creatures.

IF if they depended on heaven for their support, they would be more religious; if they were influenced by religion, they would be less abandoned in their behaviour: thus, this seeming good act, turns to a national evil, and there is more distress amongst the poor of London, than any where in Europe; such drunkenness both in male and female, as is inconceivable to you who have never passed the channel which divides England and France; however, this last vice is

LETTER XIII.

become a national advantage; the revenue arising from spirituous liquors is so very considerable, that the ministers, having drenched the nation in debt so deeply, are reduced to be much obliged to those whose vices assist them in raising taxes for their support.

SHALL we then exclaim in praise of the sagacity of that minister, who converts the sins of the people to the advantage of the whole; or shall we pity that nation whose health, morality, and religion, are duped to the pernicious schemes of destructive men, and whose vices cannot be corrected, left they and the revenue suffer. I am,

Yours.

LETTER XIII.

To the Reverend Father LORENZO FRANCIOSINI *at* Rome.

Dear Sir,

NOTHING is more the ridicule of the people of this nation, than that set of idle drones, as they are pleased to denominate those men, who, dedicated to the good of mankind, give themselves up to the service of religion; they despise from their souls, a people who can suffer such useless members in a nation, beings who live on the toil and labour of other men.

I shall not enter into a vindication of these pious men, the reflections of protestants do not affect them, and you and I want no conviction of their utility.

ALL that I shall remark is, that the sole objection to them arises from their being devoted to religion; change that name, and as great a proof of weakness is to be found amongst these sharp-sighted philosophers of England.

FOR

For inftance, put fine-cure places and trade in the room of religion, and Eaft India company in that of monks, and it will appear that the people of England are at prefent greater dupes to the Eaft India Directors, than ever they have been to the clergy at any time.

In the moft reigning hour of the catholic religion, when the clergy had fuch great poffeffions and power, the money which came into their hands remained in the kingdom, the poor and many others received affiftance from it; it is certain thefe churchmen lived in great affluence and fplendor at that time.

At prefent, the gold and filver which is gained by other trades, from the weftern world, is exported by this company for teas, china, and other ufelefs commodities; thus, the other merchants work to enrich this kingdom, and this company to impoverifh it for their own private advantage; many millions having been exported, and totally annihilated with refpect to the nation, fince the eftablifhment of this pernicious company. Is this convent of directors

LETTER XIII.

less pernicious, than those of the monks were formerly? or, is their splendor and affluence more moderate than those of the clergy? If the latter received too great a revenue, they exported less, and consequently were less prejudicial than these gentlemen in that respect.

YET such is the short-sightedness of the present administration, that this company is encouraged to the nation's ruin, and the people tamely see a set of men selected from the rest, making them their property, and wallowing in riches: unless I am misinformed, the whole profit of this trade rises from what is imported and sold to their fellow-countrymen, and not on what is carried abroad.

DOES not this appear as silly, and shew as great an infatuation, as being subjected to the artifices of Priests? and if trade was fallen into as much disgrace as religion, would it not appear as great a reflection on the understanding of a nation, to be the property of an East India director, as of a capuchin fryar? For this reason, unless the ministry, and this company, drew some reciprocal advantage different from that of of the public, this institution had long since been abolished; notwithstanding this may be the mutual advantage of the above mentioned men, it is become the people's interest to reform this power, and the abuse of it, as much at least as it was that of the power of the clergy, at the reformation; without it, as it appears to my eyes, and to those of father ******, who is well instructed in these affairs, this nation must be undone without another enemy.

If he informs me right, there have been forty millions of money coined since the restoration; of which sum there remains circulating in the hands of the natives, at the highest calculation, not more than fourteen millions, and according to some not more than twelve.

Thus, it is plain that the trade of the East Indies, and some other means which may be hereafter explained, have drained this nation continually of its cash; the pool has been running out at the lower end, as fast as it has filled from the source. Since the establishment of the East India company, this nation has only increased

LETTER XIII. 109

creafed in vifionary wealth, by jobbs and loans in time of neceffity, there being, according to fome well founded computations, as much wealth in the kingdom at the expulfion of James the fecond, as at this moment, and fcarce any taxes; the whole being no more than two millions annually levied.

The veil which covers this diminution of cafh is the bank, who lending to the minifter paper in the place of money, and it being received as fuch in all payments, conceals the efcape of that fpecie which is continually deferting this land; till at laft it will become too vifible to be unobferved, and too great to be remedied.

To fay the truth, his holinefs drew large fums of money, during the reigning of the catholic faith, from this ifland; but then the German fubfidies are as fatal at prefent, as the glory of the church was at that time; and of what confequence is it to the fubjects of this nation, whether electing and fuftaining an emperor of Germany, or a Pope at Rome, plunder them of the fruits of their labour?

The

LETTER XIII.

THE making a king of the Romans is to a Briton as ridiculous an object in itself, as recovering the holy sepulchre from the hands of the Saracens, and a crusade not more visionary, than the sustaining a ballance of power in Europe.

THE spirit of religious warfare is lost, and the latter remains to lull the people, and squeeze the money from them with less reluctance: thus this nation, however it may value itself for its being enlightened in philosophy and good sense, is in fact, all prejudice a-part, as weak in intellects, and as much subjected to delusion in the days of George the second, as before the reformation in the days of Henry the second, and Thomas à Becket; the object is changed, but the folly remains, and the latter will probably prove more fatal than the former.

FROM all I can perceive, the getting free from priests, has duped the inhabitants to East India companies, bank and South-sea directors, sine-cures of great profits, and deceits in public

LETTER XIII.

public offices; and tho' the situation of the kingdom may flatter the mole-eyed with ideas of liberty unknown to their ancestors; yet, to their ministers and their agents they are at present as great slaves, as to the kings and clergy before the reformation. I am,

Most sincerely.

LETTER XIV.

To the Reverend Father Curtio Marinelli *at* Rome.

Dear Sir,

THEOLOGISTS have adapted two manners in their accounts of providence; one that the Author of all having finished his creation; from the perfection of the creator the work must be likewise perfect, and therefore it has needed no intervening attention since its completion.

This is one way; others have supposed that tho' the creation was the work of a perfect being, yet that it requires at certain times farther superintendance and assistance from the first author.

The Britons from a self-sufficiency, ignorance, or neglect, seem to conceive their government established upon the first scheme; which

LETTER XIV.

as it is a composition of the fallibility of man, cannot be perfect, and therefore impossible.

The French, knowing what government is in its true nature, proceed on the second way of disposing things, superintend and remedy approaching evils before they become enormous.

When the people of this nation have once made a law, they imagine it will have its effect without putting it in motion, and are as careless about its execution, as if it had never been made at all; the evil proceeds, and no advantage is drawn from it.

An irregularity which cannot be totally cured is not worth their attention, the lessening inconveniencies is not an object of such all-seeing ministers; therefore because licentious and immodest women will be found in every state, no care shall be taken to diminish the mischief which they may bring; instead of being confined to particular places and prevented from seducing intoxicated men and heedless boys, they are suffered

LETTER XIV.

to patrole the streets, and spread disease every where, to the ruin of families.

In Paris and Rome there are lewd women, but they appear not in the streets; laws made in that country are observed, the people and the prince are the better for them.

Thro' the whole administration of this government, there runs a heedlessness which is not easily to be accounted for; every officer in a public place steals with impunity, and whoever thro' a design of serving his country should discover frauds of this nature, will be received with contempt, and perhaps dismissed if he has a place, whilst the thief proceeds uninterrupted.

The kingdom of Ireland has resented with justice, the countenance which has been given to a person who had robbed the public, and the minister supports the deceiver against the parliament; this may be right in this country, but would be wrong in every other.

The inhabitants of that isle are extremely loyal at present, and friends to the family on the throne; but men angry with the servants, are very apt to tranfer it to the mafter who may fupport them in their ill-deeds; at leaft, Charles the firft feems to have ruined himfelf by fomething like that conduct. Men are not beings endowed with equity fufficient to make fuch nice diftinctions, as may one day preferve the lord, and execute the fteward: minifters therefore, who trifle with themfelves, fhould take care of their mafters.

The refpect which is paid to a nation, is chiefly in proportion to the underftanding of the ruling powers, and not the money which it can raife alone; a domeftic police well directed, a care of foreign affairs that befpeaks attention and capacity in the minifter, convey to other nations that fpirit of good fenfe, which will protect a people from infults.

Yet fuch is the known relaxation of this true fpirit of government, the very Portugueze treat this kingdom with contempt; and fo little is the care in fending fit governors to their plantations, that thofe who have fhewn no marks of underſtanding in their own affairs, are ſent to direct thoſe of a people whom they know not.

By ſuch proceedings the colonies abroad are divided into feuds and ſeparate intereſts.

Besides the weakneſs of thoſe at the helm, the Engliſh have nothing to fear but the French; and yet, this ſeems the only nation againſt which they are not guarded; their ſtanding troops are not ſufficient to repell an invaſion, the paſſage is ſo ſhort from one country to another, and may be made ſo quickly in a dark night with a favourable wind, ſo little to be interrupted by the naval powers, that it is amazing no proviſion of a militia is yet inſtituted to defend this country from attacks.

One battle in the favour of the enemy will decide the fate of London; what is to be expected from a people unuſed to the thoughts of an invaſion, and untrained to arms: yet, ſuch is the remiſſneſs of the adminiſtration, that the miniſter chooſes to rely on the few troops which this nation has in pay, rather than arm the natives in their own defence, and ſeems more inclined

LETTER XIV. 117

clined that the French shall be their masters, than that they shall owe the protection of themselves and property to their own hands and virtue.

Is it a consciousness of misbehaviour which restrains him from permitting the people to be their own defenders? or, is he afraid left being indulged with the power of protecting themselves from foreign invaders, they may turn their arms on the domestic, and expell him from the presence of his master?

It is in conducting a government, as in sustaining a vast machine, the parts of the first as well as the latter must wear by action; and it is the prudence of a minister to supply those deficiencies as they come on, and thus support and continue without intermission its motion and operation: this the French continually do, they repair every failing part, and add new ones to make it yet more perfect.

The English on the contrary, inattentively let the whole machine wear out, and then are at a loss how to behave; having nothing prepared,

pared, the whole work ſtands ſtill till the new parts are made, and thus, the benefit of its motion and effect is loſt for ſome time. Indeed the French reſemble the wiſe, and this nation the fooliſh virgins in ſcripture. Since the peace of Aix la Chapelle, the Engliſh have done no one thing in favour of their nation, unleſs that of reducing the intereſt of money may be thought ſo, and which I imagine in the end will prove the contrary.

The French have proceeded on other principles, and preparing to ſtrengthen their colonies in America have built forts to ſupport them; not with deſign as is generally ſuggeſted of invading the Engliſh ſettlements at preſent, but to be in readineſs when a war ſhall be again declared between the two nations.

The colonies of Virginia and Maryland are the morſels which tempt the French appetite; the tobacco which they buy annually from the Engliſh, carries a great ſum from their nation in favour of the Britons; this they would prevent. If good authority may be relied on, the French ſcheme of going to the walls of Vienna is at an end, and thoſe of London will be their next

next attempt. If they succeed, they know their interest too well to pretend the continuing in this island, the other powers of Europe will scarce permit it. Yet, after having created universal ruin and national bankruptcy, Virginia and Maryland may be gladly given to make peace, and procure their departure.

This every Englishman in the ministerial train, tho' he saw his country invaded by a handful of Scotch highlanders, treats with infinite derision. Security, and self-sufficiency, have already ruin'd too many nations, and promises to be the bane of this.

At this very moment they are raising subsidies for electors, whose situation cannot suffer them to be their friends; the true reason of which is unknown to the subject; only to pay the interest of money, borrowed from another elector, who is the richest of the whole Germanic body, which they cannot pay themselves: Thus England is the bondsman of all the German courts, pays principal and interest, and breaks at last; busied in making a king of the Romans, and inattentive to the state of their colonies;

lonies; oppofing the French power on the continent, where it cannot hurt them, and neglecting the defence of their own country, where it is fo eafily attack'd; believing nothing can offend it, till it happens; and then totally difconcerted, thro' want of providing againft it. Such is the policy and minifterial conduct of this ifland at prefent, and fuch it will continue in all appearance. Judge what will be the event of it. I am,

Your moft obedient.

LETTER XV.

To the Reverend Father FRANCESCO SANSOVINO, *at* Rome.

Dear Sir,

THO' you have often heard of the various characters which inhabit this island, it is impossible to feign to yourself one half the oddities, which are to be found amongst the inhabitants; checked neither by religion nor policy, each runs into extremes, and the ruling whim, or reigning passion, takes up all his time, and marks his whole behaviour. From this latitudinarian manner of thinking, there is greater variety of men of the same kind, than is to be found upon the globe: the men of pleasure are all of the same stamp, in Italy and France; in this country there is some varying vein, which characterizes one from another: tho' the pursuit may be the same, yet the manner of taking and enjoying the game makes some difference in each of them.

In the law, physic, divinity, and trade, tho' there may be every where some original difference that decides to which each man belongs; yet there is some secondary distinction, which makes every man more original in this land, than is to be found in any other country.

To me, who have long resided in this isle, there start out every day new characters, which I have never seen before. Not long since two disputants in a coffee-house caught my attention; one sustained with great humour the mischief, which had been brought into the world by philosophy and learning; the other how much these studies added to the dignity of human nature: The first protested, that in his opinion there were but two useful books in the world, which were the bible and an almanac. Men, says he, cannot well do without knowing their religion and the day of the month; but as to all commentators and expositors of the scripture, they should be committed to the flames. A religion once established, should be complied with; and the object of a nation's faith once settled, should no

more

LETTER XV.

more be examined than the right of the prince, to whom a man has once sworn allegiance.

To what other purpose have all the learned theologists and philosophers published their several sentiments, but to disturb the heads of others who read their works, and believe they understand them; the last have reason'd themselves out of the truth of a small understanding, into the errors of what they think a greater, and like dwarfs who undertake to carry the burthens of giants, sink beneath the weight which becomes intolerable; they are ashamed to shew their weakness, by acknowledging that the load is too heavy for them.

What advantage have all your writers on the scriptures brought to christians, continued he; the spirit of dispute has devour'd the spirit of religion, and we want another revelation to bring back the minds of men from the various ways of thinking, and sects in christianity, as much as that revelation was necessary to destroy all the futile and clashing sects of philosophers amongst the ancients.

Out

LETTER XV.

Out of one plain truth they have produced a thousand errors, all under the sanction of infallible truth, and yet each of these truths is denied by the followers of the others: Thus, each sect being avow'd as true by some, and false by others, it comes to pass, that every sect is at once both true and false; a rare conclusion on a matter of so much consequence, as the religion of a nation. To these men of philosophy we are indebted for this absurdity; all which would have been avoided, but for these singular judgments, which differing from the vulgar, are called wise, and perhaps the least intitled to it amongst men.

I know, says he, that these wise heads and their followers assert, that the ancients permitted all opinions in their religion, and therefore had no disputes about it; but this is a mistake, the ancients of the same kingdom never differed about the genealogy or worship of their gods, nor attributed to one, what belonged to another; the worship of Jupiter was the same by all the Romans, and no one ever attempted an innovation; they never suffered it to be disputed, whether a god, received

LETTER XV.

received as such by the nation, was a god or not; or whether his temples should stand east and west, or north and south; nor would the state suffer a set of swivel-headed bigots or free-thinkers, to alter the worship of their deities, or change a national religion to please a few fanatic imaginations, perhaps of a cobler or tinker, whose impudence had thrust them into the intermeddling with the affairs of a religion.

WHAT has Locke done to human understandings, but puzzle ten thousand sculls who would have gone to their graves undisturbed but for him, and let loose millions of tongues, to prate about what they have not the least comprehension of.

SIR Isaac Newton has made more coxcombs than all the dancing-masters and mammas of London; every prig has him in his mouth, who never understood one of his problems, and nothing but demonstration can convince these gentlemen, in things even where demonstration is not to be obtained.

To

To me it seems neceſſary, that as in the affairs of gold and ſilver, there are officers eſtabliſhed to examine into the vaſes and other utenſils made of theſe metals, to ſee if they are genuine; ſo there ſhould be others, deſtin'd to inſpect and decide what underſtandings are proper to be truſted with ſuch authors, and not permit the moſt abſtruſe and difficult matters to fall into the hands of every pretender to thinking.

In my opinion, ſays he, the emperor, who burnt the library at Alexandria, was the greateſt friend to human kind; and if all the copies of Plato and Ariſtotle, as well as the other Greek and Latin writers, had been conſumed in it, we ſhould have had reaſon to bleſs the day, and paſs'd our hours in unanimity and peace. I am not ſure whether printing has not done as much miſchief as the plague.

For my part, ſays he, I would join in a petition to the legiſlature to burn all the books in the nation, except thoſe I firſt mentioned, we should have more ease, less dissipation, warmer devotion, better sense, and better times.

Thus he ended his conversation, which tho' mixt with much wildness, has yet much truth in it, and may partly serve to justify our restraining the bible from the hands of the weak and ill-judging. Adieu.

I am yours most affectionately.

LETTER XVI.

To the Reverend Father DOMINICO MANZONI, at Rome.

Dear Sir,

NOTHING has lefs truth in it than what Voltaire and abbé le Bland have faid relating to the Quakers in this kingdom : it is either plain from what the firſt has written, that he never was in their company, or did not attend to their cuſtoms. He deſcribes one of theſe gentry, with whom he dined, as taking off his hat, and aſking a benediction on his repaſt; in which he muſt be abſolutely miſtaken : it being the eſtabliſhed maxim of this ſect, never to perform that ceremony. It is the preſbyterian cuſtom indeed, to ſay a grace as long as the hundred-and-nineteenth Pſalm, before and after meals ; but a quaker aſks no bleſſing from heaven before he eats, and has not gratitude enough to return thanks after he is fill'd. To ſay the truth : the church of England does both in a becoming manner, without that ridiculous and hypocritic length, and tone, which is to be found

amongſt

LETTER XVI.

amongst the presbyterians, anabaptists and independants.

IF it was the spirit of religious enthusiasm which actuated the first Quakers; it is a spirit of another kind, which reigns amongst them at present. If simplicity of dress, and simplicity of speech, arose from the humble consideration of human nature, in the beginning; it is the love of singularity, pride, and personal advantage, which has taken possession of their hearts, and which continues their dress and manners at present.

NOTHING on this globe has half the arrogance of a Quaker; he will accost the king with Friend George, the minister with Neighbour William, and this without the least reluctance, distrust of himself, or mark of confusion. What can argue greater insolence than this of meeting those persons, whose characters all the world agree to reverence, upon equal terms, and treating them with the utmost familiarity: the son of a Quaker has more assurance at ten years old, than the wildest officer of the king's guards at twenty five.

LETTER XVI.

They call themselves Christians, but I know not what title they have to it; there is no sacrament in use in their religion: in fact, they seem to be a set of fatalists, who agree to call that cause which moves them to action, a something proceeding from the spirit. I have heard it affirmed in their company, that the resurrection of the body is not an article of their faith, if they have any at all.

As their number is but small, so they draw advantage from that circumstance, being all united in the general interest of the sect. They are almost all in trade, and therefore once in the year they meet in several towns in England, to know the state of those parts of the country: to those places of rendezvous one or more of the Quakers of the towns within two hundred miles always comes. At this time their real design of meeting is concealed, by praying and preaching; it is a religious act to the eye, but a political one at the heart; every Quaker who assembles brings the state of the trade of that town from whence he comes along with him; the particular business

of

LETTER XVI.

of every grocer, mercer, and other tradesman; his industry, manner of living, and expences: by this means the wholesale dealers of London, Bristol, and other great towns, are acquainted with the characters and business of all the tradesmen in the kingdom: they know whether their business is such as that they may be safely trusted with goods, if industry is observed in their affairs, and all other requisites for thriving in trade.

THUS the Quakers in the lesser towns and cities of England are spies on the actions of the inhabitants, and preserve their sect from losses in trade. And for this reason they endeavour to establish a Quaker in every town, if there are none already, who may bring annual intelligence.

SINGULARITY to most peoples apprehension stands in the place of merit, a gimcrack in shell-philosophy will lay out twenty guineas for a shell, which is singular and without a fellow, tho' ugly and ill-shapen; at the same time he will not give a farthing for that which has the most elegant shape and greatest diversity of colours, if the species is numerous. Thus it is not beauty, but singularity which makes it esteemed.

It is the same thing amongst men, a Quaker with his singularity of dress, behaviour, laconic style, and air of riches, the last of which he never fails to insinuate to all his customers, catches the eyes of tradesmen in the country; the apparent probity and power of selling cheap, because supposed wealthy, create him business; men in the country are desirous of talking with such a man, and thus deal with him from that singularity in him, and that whimsical disposition in themselves.

The Quakers are extremely punctual and honest in trifles, conscious that men wear out their characters before they make their fortune, who proceed otherwise in trades where riches are gotten by degrees.

But, in matters of consequence, the right of the thing is not the question; the power of obtaining it by artifice is the only object to be considered; and, if a fortune can be made at once, there is little hesitation about the manner how.

It is not a little surprising, that a set of men of such principles as the Quakers profess, could be

LETTER XVI.   133

be suffered to take root in any nation; they have covered all the political maxims which they adopt, by the veil of religion. Accordingly, in the rebellion which happened last in England, they openly avowed that their principles would not allow them to oppose it. This was nothing to be remarked in a Quaker: yet a man of the established church would have been stigmatized for a Jacobite, that had said any thing like this.

THEIR religion, it seems, will not suffer them to bear arms. What can be more ridiculous than this principle, to a man who knows human nature, except the people who indulge them in this humour?

WHAT right have any set of men to the protection of a government in times of peace, who will not assist with every power they possess to defend their country in times of war? their taxes are not greater than other peoples.

ARE the catholics more ridiculous in indulging monks amongst them without contributing to save their country by arms, than the Britons in permitting a sect amongst themselves, who

K 3   openly

LETTER XVI.

openly avow that their religion will not suffer them to defend their country?

ANOTHER indulgence their obstinacy has procured them is this; they are suffered to affirm before a magistrate that which all other subjects of this crown are obliged to depose upon oath on the Evangelists. In order to observe the effect of this sufferance, I have frequently attended trials where these people have been witnesses, and thro' the whole of my observation I have never found them give an explicit answer, when it could make against their friends; nay, the whole chicanery and search of the council could not draw an answer which was not filled with ambiguities.

THEIR cause of demanding this privilege is the most convincing reason for its not being allowed them; it is evident they imagine that there is something more obligatory, sacred and binding in an oath, than in an affirmation: therefore since all the individuals of a nation ought to be under the same influence and apprehension in the administration of an oath, it was extremely ill understood to grant this liberty of affirmation to

any

LETTER XVI.

any set of men whatever. It is a road that leads to injustice; it is injustice itself, that one man should be subjected to the terrors of eternal punishment, for the breach of that which another only conceives as something of a common nature.

THAT the legislature and the Quakers themselves conceive an affirmation to be of an inferior obligation on the person who takes it, to that of an oath, is certain: no man, whatever crime he is guilty of, can be executed on the affirmation of a Quaker; and no Quaker has refused taking his oath to the execution of one that has roused his righteous spirit, by robbing him. Thus the legislature thinks it an indulgence, and not equally obligatory, by making this difference in cases of life and death.

THE Quaker who takes the common oaths of the country, in cases of being robbed, cannot at other times plead conscience against it with justice; because either his conscience admits of doing what it knows to be wrong on these occasions, or he screens himself from what he thinks to be right

right in others, and has no real exception against.

For these reasons if he is suffered to take his affirmation in cases of property, he should not be indulged to take his oath in those of life and death. He ought to adhere to his conscience throughout, and not change the nature of the obligation as his interest and inclination permit him. In truth, it is a weakness to excuse a set of men from oaths in those instances, where all others of the kingdom are obliged to take them.

Such are the Quakers: I leave you to decide if they are that simple primitive people which Voltaire and abbé le Bland have told you; have not they found means to obtain advantages which favour of refined cunning, and secure themselves in safety whilst the nation is fighting their battles?

The celebrated system of Penn, which has been so much praised and for so little reason, is absolutely impracticable amongst men: indeed it is easy to preserve peace with the Indians, who are purchased by small presents to continue it; but can they buy off the French, who are pre-

paring

LETTER XVI.

paring to increase their dominions in America? will the spirit of meekness serve them in that case? and what has been said with respect to their indulging all religions amongst them, is not true, the catholics are excepted; and the ill effects of a general naturalization is sensibly felt amongst them, the Germans being at present so numerous that they preserve their language and interest separate, which is no small inconveniency to the country; and would as probably live under a French, as an English government.

Thus, sir, you see this applauded system of government in England and that in America is stained with as deep blots as those of other nations: it is ideally better, but in execution as bad as that of France, whose inhabitants are complimented with the name of slaves in this country.

I am yours most affectionately.

LETTER XVII.

To the Reverend Father ANTONIO COCCHI at Rome.

Dear Sir;

IT is impossible to say what may happen in this kingdom by the effect of time; but at present there is no probability of the catholic faith increasing amongst the English.

ALL public meetings but those at the ambassadors chapels are forbidden by law, the priests of our religion are not permitted to preach amongst the people, and those of an enthusiastic nature are all seized by the preachers of new sects, who harangue the multitude in fields and particular places destin'd for that end.

IT seems difficult to propagate any mode of religion amongst people who are at ease; those who feel no worldly evils are little solicited to enquire into matters of religion, they are in opulence in this world, and undisturbed about the consequences of the other: for that reason there are

are none but the poorer sort, whose distresses prompt them to follow those new preachers, who are extremely liberal in promises of rewards in heaven to those who join in their worship upon earth. A soothing consolation to the feelings of poverty!

WHAT a general calamity might effectuate, I know not; probably, as those who have no religion are the most apt to run into the opposite extreme in these situations, the catholic faith, answering fully to the dispositions of such times, might be re-established in England. At present I cannot avoid thinking, that this nation is of all others the least advantaged by the religion which is to be found in it; the heads of those who were originally designed to superintend these affairs, are either extremely weak or extravagantly negligent.

THE men in power, remiss in all things, leave this enthusiastic spirit of the field-preachers unconverted to any use, unless they suppose the weakening the established church an advantage; whereas it is capable of being turned to great national service, if they treated them as we do those

those of our religious orders, whose souls are on fire with zeal to bring their bodies to suffer for religion and the service of our church.

WERE they sent to convert the Indians in America to the christian faith, they would unite these nations more strongly to the English interest than every other power on earth; he who rules the soul, rules every thing; otherwise the French will prevail throughout the continent, whose priests are labouring to convert the American nations to their faith, and consequently to their party.

THIS being encouraged in the manner I mention, the kingdom of England would draw as much advantage from their enthusiasm in America, as it brings mischief at present in this island.

INDEED the disbelief of all futurity is so universally prevalent in this country, the men in power are altogether inattentive or ignorant what effect religion can have amongst an uncivilized and barbarous race; the short and only way they know of coming at things, is buying. This, tho' it succeeds in perfection amongst the natives, is not sure of success in other countries; and those who can prevail over the mind by objects of religion, and influence by money also, are almost sure of prevailing in the end. The French neither neglect one or the other method.

May not the reason of this ignorance in human nature be owing to this? The human heart is not so well known in this nation as in catholic countries; men judge of others by what they feel alone, and no man is various enough to found a knowledge of all mankind on what passes in himself only. Thus the man in power, directing all things from his peculiar sensations, knows little of all human nature.

In nations where the catholic religion prevails, the clergy, accustomed to attend to the various dispositions of men, by the confessions of very different tempers in head and heart, know the map of man, the shoals, creeks, bays, tides, and currents of human nature, better than those who are not acquainted with any bosom but their own: they discern what incites, and what restrains.

They

They are sensible how easily man is conducted by his ruling passion, and therefore guide it to their intentions by that way, and not break down their minds into compliance with what they please to have done, by dint of money only; by this means even the doing justly thro' a sinister influence has a vicious effect, the mind even suffers a kind of corruption in being purchased to do right.

Thus this effectual machine of zeal for the cause of God, through want of knowledge or inattention, is suffered to do mischief in this nation; which, sent into their colonies, would be productive of infinite utility. No nation knows so little how to turn the various dispositions of the heart to advantage, as the English.

No nation has more criminals condemned for violating the laws of the land than this; hundreds are transported to the plantations every year; from whence many return, and are hanged; others are servants for a certain time only.

This

LETTER XVII.

THIS brings but little advantage to the colonies; whereas, if they had encouragement given them to marry Indian women, if it made part of the judgment pafs'd on them, or the women were obliged to marry Indian men, there would then be a ftronger alliance between thefe American nations and the Englifh. Some fmall fums of money might be given on this account.

THE French practife the encouraging intermarriages between the neighbouring Indians and their people; and by this, and by their zeal for making converts, they increafe greatly in intereft amongft the Indian nations of America.

IF thefe obfervations be true, which I have received from father B—— in that country, it feems evident that riches and irreligion bring floth and ignorance in the knowledge of the human head and heart. The great fchool for the fcience of which, is at that city where you refide; where men are better known and underftood, and the different difpofitions better applied, than any where on earth; from the zealot who

who believes, burns, and dies a martyr on the fiery sands of Africa, to him who manages a nation's intereſt in the conclave. Adieu: love me, as I do you.

Your's moſt affectionately.

LETTER XVIII.

To the Reverend Father ALESSANDRO ADIMARI, *at* Rome.

Dear Sir,

HOW many things are received for certain truths by the different people of Europe, which are really without any foundation. This variety of opinions seems to me to arise from shortsightedness, or drawing paralells between kingdoms; whereas no two things in political affairs seem to be enough alike to deduce any reasonable consequence from the similarity. If you ask an Englishman, what has made arts, letters, and trade, flourish in the different parts of the world? he will immediately answer, Liberty: the Athenians were a free people; behold what prodigies the city of Athens produced; the Romans also; what did that illustrious people produce in arms, and literature! says he in rapture.

LETTER XVIII.

IN commerce, in like manner, free states alone, were those who succeeded. The Tyrians, Carthaginians, Syracusans, and Marseillians; the Genoese and Venetians; the Dutch and Brittons; what a figure have they made in the world! They have cover'd the ocean with their fleets, and brought immense riches to the inhabitants: The last of which, has not only mix'd the knowledge of trade with war, but even philosophy and science; thus it is liberty alone, which can give birth to the superior arts, superior philosophy, and learning.

IF we should grant this to be true, these assertors of this cause of learning and commerce will fall into a wilderness, difficult enough to find a path which leads from it, to safety; if we should deny it, there would be no less pain to prove the truth of this assertion.

IF painting and statuary be the works of genius, even catholic Rome has no small reason to boast of its productions in that taste; was that city then free at the times when Raphael, Michel

LETTER XVIII.

Michel Angelo, and other great men, painted and carved in it? If it was at that time, it is the same at present; the system of government being changed in no respect; this will scarce be allow'd, I fansy.

No man will deny, that the French have produced men of genius in all kinds of literature; and yet, no Englishman will allow that they are a free people; how comes it to pass, that liberty can only promote works of genius, since the French a nation of slaves, has been prolifick in those productions?

PERHAPS, in strict truth, even Rome and Athens were declining from the summit of liberty at the times of their greatest men in literary genius. If Socrates, Plato, and Xenophon, like fruit ripest just before its falling from the tree, lived in the autumn of liberty; Demosthenes, Aristotle, and others, can scarce be imagined to have past their lives in that state; or be esteem'd free in the days of Philip and Alexander: And surely Livy, Horace, Virgil, Tully, and many others

wrote

wrote in that time when liberty was no longer at Rome; to say nothing of Lucan, Tacitus, Seneca, Juvenal, and many others, who lived in the days of avow'd tyranny.

Even the greatest geniuses of this nation cannot with strict propriety be said to have lived in times when England enjoy'd its greatest freedom. The glory of England was great in the reign of Elizabeth, but the liberty was nothing in the comparison of what it has since known; surely her father's reign was not remarkable for the freedom of his subjects; and yet, Sir Thomas More lived in the days of Henry the eighth, whose little book of the Utopia has more genius in it than all those that have been written in that way.

Shakespear and Spencer wrote in the reign of Queen Elizabeth, and no men have shewn more genius in poetry than these two. Sir Walther Rawleigh, and my lord Verulam, in like manner, were far from feeling the warmest beams of liberty, and yet they are undoubtedly men of genius, particularly the latter,

who

LETTER XVIII.

who probably excell'd all men in that greatest distinction of genius, intuitive perception.

Thus it seems, that liberty is neither the cause of literature, nor genius; if it were, greater liberty would have produced greater proofs of each kind. Whereas this nation has declined in genius in many parts, since it has increased in liberty: it would be difficult to find a man of very exalted understanding in the nation at present, and yet no Englishman will allow he is not free.

Thus it is not liberty which creates genius and literature in a nation; it must then be look'd for from some other cause.

The first of these no human power, nor state, can create; it seems to be, amongst human kind, what a comet is amongst the heavenly bodies, a being, bound to no one government, that comes with superior intellects, to enlighten the understanding of this world at various times; as the other may, to replenish the orbs of this system with light, or some other qualities unknown to us.

THAT encouragement has not produced genius, is also as evidently true; since all who have ever received any advantage from superior parts, have diftinguifh'd themfelves before they were rewarded; and many a man of great capacity has languifh'd in obfcurity and penury his whole life; even thofe, whofe writings had convinced the world, that the men had merit who wrote them. It is not encouragement then which has produced the talents of thofe who are fo juftly admired.

FROM thefe confiderations perhaps it arifes, that the Englifh have appointed no ftated provifion, as an encouragement for men of fuperior genius in the polite parts of literature and fcience: The divine and lawyer are amply taken care of indeed; but the phyfician, mathematician, and others in other ftudies, have neither honors nor profits annex'd to them, for being fingularly eminent.

THE Englifh tell you, that a genius will fhew itfelf; and for this reafon it is prefumed, they conclude that the beft of thofe capacities, which

are

LETTER XVIII.

are amongst the common run of mankind, are to be neglected.

Every nation should have academies, with honor and pensions annex'd to the members of them, to call out the best exertion of those talents or degree of understanding, which every man possesses.

This, tho' it cannot make genius, will make something very near it; it will make the intellects of those who apply, more strong and ready in their studies, than those who have no incentive, but what may casually result from their labours. The mind of a student should neither be in great affluence, or in great anxiety; the first will create sloth, the other emaciate the powers of thinking, by the pain which it communicates to the soul.

Without these encouragements to study, the character of a nation will decline, and the powers also. Genius comes too rarely to support the authority of a learned people; it is therefore the business of a minister, to institute societies of that kind, where men shall be urged by honor and interest, to the discovery of things useful to the community, and preserve a nation as well as the nature of things will permit, in the rank it has acquired.

THIS the French have already done, and their academies have had the good effect of sustaining knowledge, and producing men who are of public utility to arts, sciences, trades, and manufactures. The honor of being a member of the academy of science first draws men of study to offer their observations and discoveries; which, if approved of, introduce them by degrees to be chosen members: where, after farther proofs of their abilities, they become pensioners, and are at ease enough to proceed leisurely in their studies during life.

THE great business of a nation is, to convert the common talents of men to the greatest possible advantages, not waiting the arrival of genius; which, like the Messiah to the Jews, may never come; which if it should arrive, is to be consider'd as something above expectation, and applied accordingly to their farther utility.

THIS the French know and pursue; the English, on the contrary, despise, are ignorant of,

LETTER XVIII.

of, or neglect; hence it must incontestably follow, that sooner or later France must gain the ascendant over all those who are remiss in these affairs. The spirit of invention is greatly promoted amongst all ranks of people in France, every common mechanic is rewarded with some gratuity, proportion'd to its utility; and the minister will read a memorial of any thing proposed as an advantage, without rejecting it with the ignominy of a project, and projector, even if it come from the hands of the meanest artizan or labourer; and, if it offer any thing that is probable to be carried into execution, reward him for the hint.

If commerce has not hitherto advanced much amongst any states but those which are free, it is not because a monarchic government is not fit for the support and encouragement of trade; but because monarchs having hitherto esteemed trade as something below their attention, and neglected to turn their eyes that way, conquest has been the pursuit of kings, glory in arms their chief object, till England and Holland growing great by trade, have shewn them, that there are other ways of aggrandizing

grandizing a nation, than that of extending their dominions.

In consequence of this, the French trade has proved a formidable rival to that of England; and by determining the view of their measures on this object, wean'd them from the vision of universal monarchy, and enrich'd their nation.

The monarch, who determines to take the care of commerce under his protection, has it in his power to promote it beyond that which can be expected from a free state. Good laws may be defeated by clashing interests in popular assemblies, each set of tradesmen opposing the increase of trades different from their own; perhaps the nature of a free state will scarce permit that rigour of enquiry which is necessary to keep men from committing frauds in the manufactures which they are engaged in.

The inspection of the French manufactories in every respect is so order'd, that no frauds can be committed; the minister knows the nature and pursuit of commercial men is to enrich

LETTER XVIII.

rich themselves: this desire being entirely selfish, is but little apt to consider posterity, or be strictly honest. For these reasons, those propensities are check'd by public inspection: a trade once begun with a foreign kingdom is almost certain of being establish'd, the merchandize being sure of continuing the same; the foreign merchant knows this, and depends upon it.

WHEREAS the mechanics and manufacturers of England, having no superintendancy over their productions, goaded on by the desire of sudden gain, have full licence of deceiving: For this reason they have lost their trades in some branches, and must in more, whilst they are cursing the French, for robbing them of that which they lose by their own dishonesty.

IN free countries it is difficult to preserve that subordination, which is necessary to support commerce in its greatest perfection: the encouragement of advantageous schemes, and prohibition of bad practices, are never well understood, are always tedious in execution, and the laws made in consequence of one or the other ill plan'd or imperfect.

EITHER

EITHER of these designs a monarch accomplishes by a single ordinance; the first shall be encouraged, the latter shall be destroyed; and the people, accustomed to consider things with a dependancy on their sovereign, are contented with their state, live more frugally and happy than any where else, and acquiesce with what is right.

IT seems to me therefore, that a monarchic state is the most proper for the advancement of commerce, and will at last (finding the advantage, which accrues from it) prevail over all other kinds of government. It is probable that a king will listen to the public good, beyond that of particular companies; but ministers will protect those companies, in opposition to the public good, if these can protect them from their master's and the peoples resentments.

THE consideration of what luxury effects in a nation, comes under this head of commerce also. In France, the East-India commodities, which are bought for sterling money, are sold again for sterling money, and the nation is a gainer;

LETTER XVIII.

er; England, on the contrary, sending out money, sees no return for the greatest part which it consumes at home; even the sugar colonies, only supply the people with luxury; they work a whole year, swallow their manufactories down their throats, and draw little advantage to themselves by exportation; the French making their luxury consist in elegance, and consuming their own productions, export great quantities of eastern and western goods to be run into England, exported to Hamborough, and other parts of Germany; and thus convert their foreign product to domestic utility.

It is the part of a great minister, to remedy these inconveniencies, which are growing in this kingdom where I am; but there is yet no St. John, in this desert of politics, arrived to prepare the way, and foretell the coming, of this temporal saviour, so much wanted in this nation. Adieu, believe me

Yours most affectionately.

LETTER XIX.

To the Countess of **** *at* Rome.

Madam,

YOUR enquiry in relation to the amours and gallantries of the English, will afford me no very romantic subject of displaying the various revolutions of the heart, which take place in the loves of the Italians; the French have much more of the sentimental in their general nature, than the English; their gallantries are conducted with more decency, and more time is past together between the amorous pair, than in England.

IN general, it is the extinction of desire which is the object of every Englishman's pursuit; yet, when they do love sincerely, no beings upon earth are so totally devoted to their passion as the natives of this isle; they hang, drown, and shoot themselves, if disappointed in their loves; nothing is restraint enough on their inclinations: men of the highest rank marry women of even infamy,

LETTER XIX.

infamy, not to say of extreme low birth; and ladies of noble families wed their footmen, players and singers; that universal manner of breeding children to scarce any restraint, that spirit which is ill understood for liberty, indulging them to think that all actions which are not directly criminal, are not culpable. This, tho' it will appear extremely strange to your apprehensions, is not considered so here; many women who have been public prostitutes, have figured at court with titles, by this accident of marriage.

I am apt to believe, that few beings in any nation are truly actuated by the real sensation of love; the design of meeting in the sexes, being very well answered by an inferior degree of, perhaps, a quite different passion.

In England it is considered as unmanly and effeminate to dangle after a woman, to prevail by sighs, tender speeches, long sufferings, and perseverance; to take a heart like a citadel is a thing unknown amongst them : the most decent Englishman therefore, in search of a mistress, applies where he is most probable of success,
amongst

amongſt the meaner claſs of women, who are extremely beautiful in this nation, and making a compliment of his money, which he and ſhe prefer to bleeding hearts and all amorous acknowledgements, obtains his deſires.

For theſe reaſons the power of women is infinitely leſs here, than in Italy or France.

In the public gardens, at plays, operas, and aſſemblies, here is no chichiſbe nor amant as in Italy and France, who ſighs, grins, ogles, fetches and carries like a well educated ſpaniel.

As man, madam, is a creature which is extremely fond of power, ought I not to glory in this freedom which an Engliſhman preſerves, in thus keeping independant of the thraldom of beauty, and its ſervice, which is ſometimes very ſeverely exacted?

Yet, ſuch is the ſenſation of true love, that I would renounce all other enjoyments on earth to poſſeſs the object, and feel that thrilling paſſion which I once knew; to ſee the emanations of reciprocal delight darting from the eyes of

her

LETTER XIX.

her whom I adored; our whole souls corresponding to each other's touch, like strings in unison; for surely souls have power of touching each other; the joy of being ever with her, and she impatient of my absence, whether in the moment of exalted rapture, or in the chilling hour which generally succeeds, alike ardently desiring to be consubstantiated with her.

This, in spite of vows and prayers possessed my soul entirely; this you knew and indulged the weakness for the sake of the perfection in the object; this rapture you will yet indulge; alas! distance has not yet reclaimed my heart; one thought of love and woman, brings her back in full power upon my bosom, and I am dejected whole hours after it.

As there is an indelicacy in the men of England, and as their passions are not of the most refined sort, I do not wonder that they indulge themselves with taking girls from the lower classes, which are extremely beautiful, provided they had yet been unpolluted; but such is the indelicate taste of many of the nobility and gentry of this nation, they keep expensively women as well known,

known, and as much hackney'd, as the Appian way in Italy; this is such a taste as seems not to be accounted for; they are mere hounds in their appetites, and prefer carrion to the most exquisite delicacies of the table.

I HAVE been often led to imagine, that the sultans of the east, are actuated by more delicate emotions than the northern nations; it cannot be the mere desire between the sexes, which can thus seclude them from the conversation of the world in company with women, it must certainly be that refined sensation which I yet feel; perhaps, even more exalted and refined by the warmer suns, and the temperament which reigns amongst that people.

IF it be that joy, how ill-judging is human nature, that, unconscious of the transport, condemns this slothful and unambitious life, as much to be preferred to those tumultous joys of men in full liberty, as all that has been imagined of angelic natures and their enjoyments, is superior to those of the most debased of the human kind.

THE

LETTER XIX.

THE recalling what I would ever wish to forget, has disabled me from pursuing my account of the English ladies; I feel something at my heart which so enfeebles me, that I cannot proceed; alas! after so many years of absence, I am obliged to sigh and weep myself into tranquillity. I am,

*Your most obedient
and most humble servant.*

LETTER XX.

To the Marchioness of ***** *at* Rome.

Dear Madam,

THAT women have separate delights from those of a husband's company, is nothing surprising to an Italian; but that there should be so little conversation between men and their wives when they are not disagreeable to each other, is somewhat singular. It is no uncommon thing in London, perhaps it is the most common, for a couple to live together on very good terms, who have not the least real love for each other; if their condition of life supplies them with money enough, each pursues their separate pleasures; he passes his evening at the tavern in wine, and smoaking tobacco, she drinks her afternoon's tea in chatting with her neighbour about her husband's business, her new cloaths, or any cursory tittle-tattle of the day.

AT night they tumble into one bed together, he drenched in wine, and stinking of tobacco,

LETTER XX.

bacco, she careless of this violation of decency, till next morning, when each wakes to their daily employments, and the day goes on like every other: if this prevailed only amongst those of the lowest order of human creatures, the surprize would be nothing; but citizens of great wealth, and gentlemen of great estates, pass their lives in this filthy manner; a wife who should have delicacy enough to leave her husband's bed on this account, would be considered as a woman of a vicious disposition, and be treated something like a prostitute perhaps; thus there is no kind of delicacy on either side, as they came together for some worldly advantage, so when either dies, the survivor makes a handsome funeral, and looks out for another partner.

THE widow, if she has the good fortune to outlive the good-man, wears her weeds a whole year, and sighs heavily every hour after a new husband; so indelicate are the women of this country, even those that are still thought modest, they never restrain themselves to any number of husbands, and meet one with as much indifference, or joy, as they met the other, even to half a dozen.

THIS kind of behaviour is not to be found in Italy; women who marry men for their conveniency, seldom bear their company with good temper, tho' divested of all these displeasing sensations which accompany wine and tobacco; and in France one bed never contains such a pair; she that has lost the man she loves, is never indifferent, much less happy, with another after the first is no more.

PRAY Madam, tell me, you who know the human heart better than any philosopher I have read, or been acquainted with, is this want of delicacy in these people a real loss of happiness, or is it not?

FOR my own part, I am convinced, that in this kingdom it is not, as far as my observation can extend.

HUMAN souls of a superior nature, like the most elegant and best formed instruments, are easier put out of tune, than those of a coarser fabric; a dust, lying on a particular part, shall impair the sound of one; and a trifle disturb the

LETTER XX.

repose of the other; a rainy day untunes both: tho' the harmony of the instrument is most exquisite, and the delights of the mind ineffable, yet considering how many disagreeable accidents are probable to arrive, which may discompose one and the other, is it not better to be formed of less delicate materials, and, tho' wanting the the highest excellence in sound or sensation, to possess a common fiddle, or a common soul?

To carry on the allusion; if we could always play solos, happiness might be obtained by those of refined tastes; but as society is almost necessary to our natures, and each sex thinks itself unhappy to a certain degree, till united with the other, as greater pieces of music composed of many parts, are necessary to shew all the powers of harmony; so perhaps, the probability of meeting with corresponding tempers and according tones makes it better to have less delicate sensations, and being less pleased with one another, feel no misery from jarring dispositions.

The ladies of the best quality are indeed relieved from this cruel manner, which prevailed not long since, amongst the nobility even, when drinking and smoaking were more the custom than at present: notwithstanding this change, and that the ladies are more in company with men than usual; yet, they have not all the sweetness of temper, which so truly characterizes a woman. That freedom which French education gives the females of Paris, so artful in fact, and yet so artless in appearance, is not yet arrived in this capital, but in few families; like the first flight of woodcocks but here and there one, which, like all scarce things, are much valued and difficultly met with.

GALLANTRY in England is not understood, and complaisance to the opinion of women has not yet prevailed enough to make their opinions in literature fashionable; it is not that their understandings are not as good as in any part of Europe, but the ladies themselves have not yet taken upon them to determine in works of literature, and writers think themselves above being criticised by female remarks.

IN this they are wrong, in my opinion; I would rather take your judgment in matters of

polite

LETTER XX.

polite writing, than the firſt wit's of Italy, and ſhould think myſelf ſafer in your approbation, than in that of a long liſt of literati, whom I could mention. Women have in general more delicate ſenſations than men; what touches them is, for the moſt part, true in nature; whereas men, warpt by education, judge amiſs from previous prejudice, and referring all things to the model of the ancients, condemn that by compariſon, where no true ſimilitude ought to be expected.

I wish ſincerely you could travel to this kingdom, and ſpeak this language: how proud ſhould I be to ſee you preſide at your aſſembly of men of letters, ſoothing the Engliſh to politeneſs by your preſiding genius, and letting them ſee what advantage one polite woman would bring to all their literary productions.

I am ſtill flattering myſelf, the day will come, when women will have the aſcendant, and take to their protection the languiſhing arts, and expiring letters. Tho' I am not a native of this land, yet I own long reſidence amongſt

the

the inhabitants, and the fame they have juſtly merited in learning, makes me wiſh that ſome auſpicious hour would arrive, and retrieve the declining ſtate of literature. I am,

Your moſt obedient ſervant.

LETTER XXI.

To the Reverend Father BATISTA GUARINI, *at* Rome.

Dear Sir,

WE have it from more than human authority, that a prophet has no honour in his own country; in like manner, to keep the character of a people in its fullest lustre, it should never be seen. A nation reputed for learning and philosophy, when we read at a distance the authors it has produced, fills us with admiration; we forget to imagine, that every one in it is not a man of letters and science, and entertain conceptions which are much above nature; yet, when it comes to be beheld, we soon find our mistake: a whole people, like an individual, loses admiration by acquaintance.

To you, who live on the other side of the Alps, who study Newton, and adore him, all England appears fill'd with such geniuses. But

But what will you say, when I tell you, that the reigning philosophy at present, is, collecting natural curiosities, fossils, shells, and petrefactions of all kinds; and mathematics much neglected. It is much easier to remember all the different kinds of natural productions, than to solve a problem in the abstruse mathematics; for one, who can perform the latter, there are thousands, who are equal to the first. Whoever has memory enough to retain the names, and patience sufficient to gaze till he knows one production from another, is an adept in that philosophy. Thus, the number is increased, and the value lessened.

You would be amazed to see how degenerate this nation is become: can you conceive, that in the land where Bacon and Newton were born, there should not be one extensive genius, or one considerable mathematician. The academy of science at Paris, at present, has much greater men in that study, than are to be found here: Clairaut and d'Alembert are superior to Simson, who is almost the only one which belongs to the royal society.

Indeed,

Indeed, to the honour of England, here is one nobleman, who is by much the greateſt mathematician in the world, amongſt men of high rank; it is my lord Stanhope.

At the meetings of theſe philoſophers, gazing with raptures at a cockle-ſhell of a new kind, admiring the aptitude with which each animal is fitted to his deſtination in nature, wondering at the humming-bird and his neſt, built with ſo much art, and inſtinct; I have beheld them with the utmoſt contempt; conſcious that their intellects were not ſtrong enough to ſee the fitneſs of religion to human kind.

These wondrous philoſophers, who extoll the ſupreme intelligence ſo highly in the ſtructure and diſpoſition of a fly, ſmile at the word miracle; and from mere poverty of genius conceive that to be falſe which is unintelligible to their limited capacities. When alas! the wings of that insect are not more adapted to the uſe of flying, than miracles are to faith in man; and as inſeparable from his well-being, and his nature.

There

LETTER XXI.

THERE is a certain kind of capacity, which is not exalted enough to see that human nature is imperfect in all its researches, nor humble enough to acknowledge its incapacity, which is destructive to itself, and intolerable to men of great understanding; prompt to examine all things, and capable of comprehending none, as it ought; it begets an arrogance in full health, which terminates in uneasiness in old age; such is that of the philosophers of this present hour in Great Britain.

IF you mention the attributes of the deity, each of them shall descant an hour on his infinite wisdom, justice, and benevolence; and if you name the christian religion, they will give you to understand, they do not believe one word of it to be true: How incompatible with the former part of their conversation is this last declaration? How short-sighted is this pretension to philosophy? Infinite wisdom, justice, and benevolence, have suffered mankind to be govern'd seventeen hundred and fifty years by a rule and guide, which has not a word of truth in it.

THIS

This is either making their deity impotent, or regardless of the welfare of his creatures (neither of which can be deduced from their principles) and destroys his attributes.

Is there one man amongst them, who has yet assign'd from what cause one part of his favourite shell is white, the other purple; he must tell you, nature made it, and the eye sees it so; it is taken off intuitively. If he should ask a believer, why he gives credit to miracles? He would answer: God ordain'd them, and his faith was convinced of the truth of them: At this the philosopher would laugh, and yet the humbler man of faith has all to urge in his favour, that this mighty man of reason can plead for himself; the one tells you the colours are so to his eye; the other, that the transactions are so to his faith, and all the reasoning on earth upon either of them would be exactly equal; neither of them being able to explain, how the shell became purple and white, nor how water became wine. One has the evidence of sense to convince him, and the other the evidence of faith to convince him; and the world
acquiesce

acquiesce alike in both, where nature has been uncorrupted by false philosophy, and delusive pretensions to thinking and research.

Methinks there is nothing so truly great in the character of Socrates, as despising all knowledge which did not tend to the study and discovery of human nature: even the sublimer parts of philosophy, the inquiry into the motions, connections, and dependances of the heavenly bodies, which require genius and application, are infinitely inferiour to that of the studying man. What would that divine philosopher have said of those, whose whole pursuit is amassing together the scarce and rare productions of nature, whose happiness consists in having a shell which no man else possesses, neglecting all application to useful knowledge.

These philosophers, like the reasoning of the sophists of old, are productive of evil to science and mankind; they bring a contempt on the appellation, in the opinion of many, which extends itself over other parts of what is distinguish'd by that name, or creating a real character and valuation in the heads of others,

for

LETTER XXI. 177

for such trifles, seduce them from more reasonable and worthy pursuits, and lessen the true value of real knowledge.

ALMOST all of this stamp, are proud in being esteem'd unbelievers; yet it is remarkable, that the most extensive capacities have been christians; Sir Isaac, and Mr. Locke, are known to have been such, but these men are wiser; they have discover'd the secret behind the curtain, and being too cunning to be deluded by the falacy and art of priests, are only dupes to their own weakness and follies, a kind of *felones de se*, who have the great consolation of destroying their happiness by their own wrong reasoning, as the others have their lives by their own rash hands.

I HAVE often imagined, that amongst men there are to be found all kinds and degrees of knowledge, which heaven has given to the other animals of the creation; the men of this kind of understanding, resemble moles, who have just sense enough to grovel in the dirt, and discern fossils, it is their native sphere; but when they emerge into day-light, are astonish'd, and judge

VOL. I. N amiss,

amifs, from the imperfection of their organs, and full blaze of truth.

If a man would attend to the fenfations which pafs in his own bofom, and unravel the combination of thofe materials, with which he is compofed, without flattering the vanity that prompts him within, he will perceive, at leaft, I perceive it myfelf, that there are moments, hours, and days, when reafon has no influence in correcting the difquietude we feel, where the only folid rock, which offers us a firm footing, is the belief in the mediation of a celeftial advocate, and redeemer of mankind; when the objects of religion only take place, and foothe the mind to a contentment with itfelf.

Can thefe feeble philofophers calculate, how many animals are contained in a drop of fluid, admire how nicely the form of every creature is adapted to its exercife and employment, and not remark how truly the objects of religion are adjufted to the various fabric of the foul of man; even the belief of a Mediator and Redeemer, are fuch confolatory ideas, so fitted to the wants of human nature, that, were there no other testimonies and advantages in the christian doctrine, I should declare, that revelation came from heaven. Is honey and wax more natural and necessary to the bee, than such expectations and dependance to human kind? Is that insect better formed for collecting these productions, than the mind of man for receiving the succour and belief of such opinions? Is it reasoning like man, to admire the formation of a bee, and exclaim there is a God, and then seeing the means, by which he has ever conducted mankind, assert there is none?

Such it is at the conclusion: if religion is an absurdity, it is not one of those transient things, which seem to obstruct or interfere with the general proceedings of providence, like earthquakes or plagues. It is a stable being, the standard rule and direction of man's behaviour: either religion is therefore of his hand and revelation, or there is no God. For to suppose man governed eternally by a falsehood, is to suppose that there is no superintending

tending power. If they perfift to affert, that there is that power, from the works of the creation, from flies and infects, which directs them by inftinct to what is right, and deny the truth of religion; they own that there is a god of flies, and not of men; that the bee, and ant, are objects of his care, and man left unheeded and uncared for; either a partial deity, or oppofed by fome malevolent power, which reftrains him from the exertion of his will.

THE ruling philofophy of France is more confentaneous to itfelf, than this in England: the materialifts found all thefe phænomena in mental nature, as arifing from matter alone; and tho' there have yet appeared no philofophers amongft them, who have traced the circulation of things, thro' the whole round of what is call'd caufe and effect, yet they affign all alike to one material caufe, and are not fo weak and contradictory to imagine, that there is a being who prefides over infects, and is inattentive to what paffes amongft men.

IT

It is generally said, that there never was a speculative Atheist; whether there ever have been such men or not, I shall not take upon me to decide; yet, I am convinced that I could with more ease be induced to follow that philosophy which supposes the cause of all things to exist in their own nature; that is, that the different degrees of subtilty in matter, and the affections of its various parts, attracting and repelling, are equal to the production of all the phænomena which we behold in nature, than acknowledging a providence, which has formed and presides over all, exclude him from the superintendancy of human kind, giving him as a god of flies and insects, and permitting man to be guided by something totally erroneous. This last manner of conceiving things, is that generally received by those who deal in the knowledge of shells, and are unjustly named deists; the philosophers of England.

The other system of materialism, is the modish philosophy of France. I am neither the

the follower of one or the other; but taking nature as she appears, am convinced that there is a God of insects and of men.

ADIEU, remember me in your address to that being.

I am your most obedient.

LETTER XXII.

To the Reverend Father FABIO MARETTI *at* Rome.

Dear Sir,

AFTER the found of an inftrument has been communicated to a place of echoes, there remains a long while fome dying tone which the ear diftinguifhes, that makes it regret the lofs of the mufic which imparted it.

IN like manner, the languid ftate of letters in this nation imparts a pain to thofe who afpire to be received of that number; they remember like a fine woman the full funfhine of their beauty, and knowing that they are ftill agreeable, cannot bear being treated with flight in the declining hour, when the fhadows are largeft.

AT prefent, all attention is turned from fenfe to found, and an Italian fiddler of note coming from Rome, would find admission and countenance, where a genius equal to Horace, travelling from the same place, would meet no reception.

Music is the fashionable favourite of the ladies; a fiddler is received in this country as an emissary from the skies; and I am convinced, if the ladies were to order a picture of our Saviour's being received into heaven, they would follow the Dutch taste, only instead of angels playing on the violin, they would think to honor him more by the company of Italian fiddlers.

One of these gentlemen is considered of consequence enough, to divide a nation into two parties in his favour. The distinction of Whig and Tory is almost at an end, and the concertists and operasts will probably take their place with equal vehemence; for this nation must be divided by something.

The money which these performers get in this city is amazing; they are no longer considered as creatures of entertainment, but rank;

LETTER XXII.

they keep better company than men of letters, and often very arrogantly refuse playing at the houses of great men where they have dined; how would an Italian nobleman consider such behaviour?

So much sound has gained on sense, and the talents of one performer obtained upon those of the other, that for one who sighs after the genius of Shakespear, there are thousands who pant with desire to play like Digardino; and so much he profits of his skill, that I believe myself but little mistaken, when I assert, that he gets as much money by his violin, as the whole number of writers in the kingdom do by their knowledge. This will in a great measure explain the reason of their being more enamoured of sounds, than understanding; and preferring the modulations of an artful musician, to the finest productions of the most vivid and just imagination.

Perhaps, the security which attends criticism on music, is the great cause of its being promoted by the patrons of fiddlers; there are no treatises written on the composition of concertos,

LETTER XXII.

certos, trios, overtures, and folos, as there are on heroic poems, tragedy, comedy, paftoral, elegy, and fatire; thefe, tho' they never impart tafte, furnifh rules which the people of pretenfion to literature apply; with thefe they combat the opinions of thofe who have never read them, tho' probably of better tafte, and make their judgment controverted.

In mufic tafte is more arbitrary; and if a lady who has travelled into Italy, who does not know one note in the gamut, or when an inftrument is in or out of tune, talks much of the Cantabile and Cromatic, fhe fhall be efteemed a fpirit of choice difcernment in harmonic knowledge, and followed as blindly as the oracles which the prieftefs of the god of mufic delivered to his votaries of old.

I have known more than one inftance of this, I affure you, where a lady has been dying in raptures at the found of a fiddle, that was fqueaking out of tune, and the upper part of the compofition had no more mufic in it, than the whetting a knife, filing a faw, or the crying of a fow hung by the head in the ftye; at

the

the same time, nine parts in ten of the company screwing faces in concert and complaisance to her ladyship, which would have made a study or academy for artists who carved heads of sticks, or paint in Caracatura.

It is amazing in all countries, how much pretension to taste finds means of dissipating, but no where more remarkable than in England; here are men of fortune who sacrifice a thousand pounds in exhibiting a tragedy, only to convince the world how ill they are made for the representation of great things.

Many a man of quality entertains the world with concerts, to shew that of the thousand requisites which are necessary to make a complete fiddler, he wants but two, stopping in tune, and playing in time; however, there was yet a more extraordinary reason which induced an English Jew who resided at Paris, to give a public concert, which was to shew, that his lady's gallant was not an eunuch, for no human head could divine to what other intent he was desired to sing.

LETTER XXII.

It is become the fashion in this city to procure charities by musick; that power has found the way of aiding in the support of hospitals, melting from hearts as hard as stone, the sum of one guinea for a concert ticket. I imagine Amphion was an Italian fiddler, and the walls of Thebes were built much in this manner, perhaps by subscription concerts; I think operas were not then in fashion, that insipid taste of chanting frigid nonsense, thro' three acts, is an invention of the moderns, and owes its rise to our nation:

The genius of the English is not much turned for music, tho' much more so than that of France, fashion makes its present prevalency; the conversation which is continued at concerts whilst the finest pieces are performing, puts this remark beyond contradiction; or, it must be a strange degree of self-love, which prefers the sound of its own voice, to the finest compositions of Corelli, Handel, or Geminiani.

Notwithstanding the protection and encouragement which are given to the natives of our country, I should with pleasure see the revival

vival of letters, and the languid flame of science cherished by that generous fuel, which it merits from the attention of great men; when it happens, I shall not fail of communicating it to your knowledge. Adieu, believe me,

Yours affectionately.

LETTER XXIII.

To the Reverend Father ANTONIO COCCHI *at* Rome.

Dear Sir,

THERE is nothing which the English value themselves more upon, than their being free from those slavish apprehensions, to which superstition subjects the minds of men in catholic countries; they are continually deriding our belief in the power of saints, and wonder how human creatures can be so weak, as to give credit to their influence and efficacy.

To a new comer, this looks so much like a nation of philosophers, that it is no wonder, strangers have reported such favourable ideas, in their accounts of this people; and yet acquaintance brings down all this apparent superiority, to the level of that in other nations; indeed, they do not believe that the shrine of St. Francis, or St. Anthony, the Virgin's or saints relicks,

LETTER XXIII.

relicks, have any power of doing miraculous cures; but they believe, that one medicine can dissipate all diseases, and that a horse-shoe nailed on the threshold of the door, will keep all evil beings from the house.

Even the people of condition yield to this faith in quack remedies, and put their lives into the hands of ignorance itself: owing to this credulity in the people of this island, it is, that so many remedies of infallible virtue, are constantly advertised against all the evils which can affect the human body. In looking over the public papers, one would imagine, that the avenues of death were intirely stopt, and his realms in danger of receiving no more subjects; yet, such is the event, that thousands find a speedier way to that kingdom, by these preventives.

How is the belief in one universal remedy founded in truth, beyond that of believing in the powers of saints; is it not equally the effect of enthusiasm or superstition? from the first, if the mind of the person affected is naturally inclined to hope, and from the latter, if inclined to fear; the love of life, and fear of death produce both.

In

LETTER XXIII.

IN truth, it is as reasonable to believe, that the effluvia breathing from the shrine which inclofes the relicks of St. Francis, can cure any difeafe, as that a drop or pill of the fame nature, can cure two difeafes fpringing from two different caufes, or a thoufand from fo many caufes, if fo many can fubfift.

WHERE is the greater ridicule in believing in one, more than another? or is the contempt of fuperftition and enthufiafm, better founded in the Englifh, than in the Italians? what philofophy is there in believing impoffibilities in medicine, more than in religion?

THUS then, the nature of the object is changed in this kingdom, but the paffions which receive them remain; and the habits moft prevalent in each country, make each purfuit feem lefs contradictory to good fenfe.

IN fact, it is the nature of the human heart to be anxious in ficknefs, and the head to be eafily prevailed on, by its perfwafive fenfations;

for

LETTER XXIII.

for that reason, in religious countries the diseased flies to his saint for safety and protection; and in those who have none, to quack medicines; each believes, that one and the other has some inexplicable power of extirpating their grievance, and the believer in universal remedies, is as much a superstitious devotee, as he that confides in St. Anthony.

PRAY, is it more incredible that St Anthony preached to the fishes, and that they attended his discourse, than that a minister has found a way to preach men into the ruin of themselves and posterity; or, that he can conceive it possible to oppose the invasion of an enemy of regular troops, with those who never knew the use of arms; yet, the latter is true to my certain knowledge.

Mr. Addison treats with much ridicule, the believing that an image of our lady in Italy changed the position of our Saviour from one arm to another, to preserve it from injury; and yet his countrymen have believed as improbable things within this last year.

LETTER XXIII.

THE favourers of a girl who had sworn a robbery against an old woman, and was afterwards convicted of perjury, believed that this girl lived a month upon one pound of bread and a small pitcher of water, without diminution of strength; and that the old woman was at one and the same time in two different places, more than a hundred miles distant from each other; for this must be their belief, the old woman being proved beyond all contradiction to be at that distance, at the time when the other swore that this robbery was committed, and the advocates of the girl believed she was present at the robbery.

PRAY, what is there more ridiculous in the Virgin's power of changing postures with the child, than in an old woman's being at two places at one and the same minute; or, how are the Italians more ridiculous in the belief of the first, than the English in that of the latter; I am convinced, that for one Italian who believes the story of the virgin, there are twenty English who believe this of the girl and the old woman, and people of a rank where one should not expect such absurd
credulity:

LETTER XXIII.

credulity: indeed the whole nation was divided on this ridiculous story of the old woman and girl, with as much zeal, as if their whole fate depended on it.

THUS then, the credulity of a nation may be as visible and easily duped, where religion does not afford it objects, as where it does; and if the church does not find it proper diet, it will take it for itself.

I HAVE often smiled at the account which Dr. Middleton has given, of the conformity between pagan and catholic Rome in matters of religion; a discovery made long before his time, and acknowledged by our writers; it is just as ingenious as it would be to prove the conformity between the functions of the body of those men who lived in the time of Numa, and pope Leo the tenth.

A PHILOSOPHER who knows his proper object, does not admire at, or condemn this conformity, he is convinced that human nature is still the same in all countries; that the mind actuated

actuated with religion cannot avoid shewing marks of gratitude, and being pleased with seeing the object of their adoration served with incense, pomp, and splendour. To what purpose is all this satire against votive pieces, lighted tapers, burning perfumes, and other ceremonies of this kind; the minds of these people are only incited by gratitude, to actions of adoration and devotion in these objects of the senses; it changes not essentials in our religion, and those creatures are not capable of being led by reasoning, to the paths which conduct to happiness.

Every Englishman would be a philosopher, and treat mankind as beings influenced by reasonable motives only; than which nothing shews a greater deficiency in true philosophy: the effect of which is, that the common people neglected, and uninfluenced by objects of the senses, are untouched by any power of religion, and totally abandoned, as one hour's ramble in the streets of London will convince the most incredulous.

Is it wiser then, to ridicule and despise the resemblances which he has recited in his epistle, and

LETTER XXIII.

leave the populace unreſtrained, than to hold their minds ſteady to their duty, by ceremonies which can have no ill tendency? As a philoſopher, Dr. Middleton muſt have agreed in the latter, and as a chriſtian he ought to have ſaid nothing, becauſe he felt no influence from that faith, it may be juſtly preſumed from his other works. I am,

Your's moſt affectionately.

LETTER XXIV.

To the Reverend Father DOMINICO MANZONI, at Rome.

Dear Sir,

I AM apt to believe from what may be seen amongst this people, that the love of riches always brings the ruin of a nation with it, not by the luxury, which is for the most part the consequence of that desire, but from weaning the mind from every other pursuit.

THE souls of those people, who are actuated by this passion, are eternally separating more and more from the universal mass; they resemble the ground which cleaves into distinct parts, and becomes sterile by too much driness; it is thirsty, and would rob all other parts of their native dividend of moisture.

NOTHING

LETTER XXIV.

Nothing should be so much guarded against by a legislator, as the evil effects of this love of money; this nothing can effectually do, but an universal belief of a future state; a day of answering for all crimes by punishment, and receiving full reward for virtue.

The system of every legislator must be imperfect for ever, without this. No plan of government, however excellent in preventive and penal laws, can answer that design. Men may be guilty of the most infamous transactions, where no part of them can be known, but to themselves, against which the fear of corporal punishment cannot effectuate any thing, and from the steady belief of religious obligation alone, any effectual check to vice, or impulse to virtue, can be expected. Self-love in this transient state, must be overcome by the self-love in that of Eternity. Therefore all those appear to be drivelers in philosophy and man, who would weaken the influence of the rewards and punishments of another world; can it

be

be too much encouraged to virtue, or withheld from vice by any motives? and if punishment be not everlasting, the reward which attends virtue cannot be intitled to it, becaufe each relating alike to the commiffion of temporary evil, and temporary good, the recompence for virtue has no title to eternal rewards, more than that of vice to ever-during punifhment. Thus, what the libertine gains by fuppofing the punifhment is not eternal in the other world, the pious and devout foul lofes by the thoughts of his happinefs being limited in its duration, when this life is at an end: at the fame time, motives to virtue are enfeebled on both fides the queftion, by fuftaining, that punifhment hereafter cannot be everlafting, and the two moft animating paffions of the human heart, are leffen'd in their force and operation, hope, and fear.

THE truth of this is manifeftly feen in the practice of all the common people of this city.

ONE would be led to imagine, that it was the avow'd fcheme of the miniftry in this kingdom,

to

LETTER XXIV.

to deftroy all incentive to virtue, or reftraint from vice. Every man that is not of the eftablifh'd church, is obliged to take the facrament as an oath of his conformity to it, before he can accept any office under the government; not that they who oblige him, expect he fhould keep it any more, than he intends adhering to this moft facred obligation, at the moment of his taking it.

By this action, the minds of men being robb'd of that uniting principle of integrity, which holds them firmly together, are more eafily invaded by all future attacks from the fide of intereft, and open to corruption; the firft breach makes way for the inroad of every fucceeding vice.

The common people of London, who are indeed fubjected to no powers, but the fecular, are moft heinous inftances of the mifchiefs which the neglect of religious motives brings on a nation. There is at prefent nothing however, impoffible according to the rules of common nature, that numberlefs witneffes may not be

brought

brought to swear for small sums of money; every trial gives instances shocking to human nature, of this contempt of the name of God.

The regard paid to money, being the only thing consider'd as essentially good amongst the greatest, without regard to the perfections, or excellencies of the mind, it is become a received maxim, that by whatever means riches can be obtain'd, possession obliterates all shame belonging to it.

Thus the terrors of another world being totally annihilated, the most monstrous crimes are every day committed; the effect of the fear of death in these instances is lost, and that strong restraint from evil, so natural to human minds, the pain of shame, is totally eradicated.

What sting has death to those who never reflect on futurity, and live unhappy lives? What punishment is shame to souls, which have lost the sense of it.

The

LETTER XXIV.

THE two great engines of government in this kingdom, are render'd useless, religion, and the sense of shame: to so detestable a degree the affair of perjury is arrived, that the legislator, who ought to make and preserve laws against that most destructive of all evils to human society, is the very person who bribes them to that iniquity; the very means which lead to the obtaining the highest honors are prostituting the minds of the electors to the guilt of perjury. If ministers are to answer for the good they omit doing; what have those to answer, who are destoying all distinction between *fas* and *nefas*; considerations of the highest import to the well-being of mankind.

THEY exclaim vehemently against ruling the mind by religious awe, it is all superstition and slavery; the catholic potentates, who keep men to their duty, by the influence of priests and church-power, are all a set of most infamous men; it is a tyranny over the conscience, which a free agent should not bear; a flagitious practice of stripping and deluding the

the poor people of their effects, and right of thinking for themselves.

THIS has been the constant cry ever since the revolution; but is it a national good, or more honest and virtuous in a minister to destroy all obligation from religion, and setting the kingdom loose from the regards which it owes to heaven and earth; putrify the minds of a whole people, by the taint of one universal bribery, and corruption.

IF in Italy their governors keep mankind too strict to their duty, and more in subjection than they ought; if the fears and hopes of futurity influence too much, and subject them to their ecclesiastical power beyond what nature can bear and be easy, and liberty is too much infringed by restraints; there is yet a million times more mischief done in this country, by the whole bond of human nature being broken, and men encouraged by public bribery, to the commission of that which corrupts the mind entirely.

LETTER XXIV.

If liberty confift in the fecurity of property, what fecurity can any man have for what he poffeffes, or for his own life, when perjury is openly encouraged? Will thofe who are guilty of avow'd and public perjuries, once in feven years, be men of integrity all the other intervening time? Liberty therefore is more infringed by this habitude of licentious indulgence, than by all the reftraint from ecclefiaftic power; the fole difference lies in this: the natives of England think that the Italians are cajoled into flavery, and lofs of their property, by priefts; and here the minifter buys them like oxen in the market, to their own flaughter. The latter may be more pleafing, but the people are flaves alike.

This is the prefent mode of ruling in England; and from fuch proceedings, what can be expected, but goals fill'd with felons; highways and public ftreets fwarming with thieves and beggars, and the gallows groaning beneath the crowds of thofe that are executed: the minifters firft try every way to take off the effects

fects of shame, and fear of death, and then wonder that men plunder and are hang'd.

A DAY of execution here is attended with as much pleasure, as a shew of gladiators was in old Rome; the contempt of death is as much applauded by the populace in this action as in the other, or *si sic pro patria concidisset*: It communicates no more terror to the spectators, than the slaughtering a bull. The frequency of the celebration of the hanging-feast, as it is call'd, has made it as little aweful as the felling dead sheep in the shambles; the populace have rank'd it amongst the diseases of life, and think it no more unnatural to die of a rope and an executioner, than of a doctor and a fever.

PERHAPS you will be apt to impute much of this cause to neglect in the clergy of this country; some there may be, but the cry against the church-power is so great, and the sin of popery so readily imputed to those who would do their duty this way, by the dissenters, that I know not, whether they may with safety set about an innovation of this kind.

NOTHING is more amazing to my apprehension, than that a nation which has struggled

LETTER XXIV.

so nobly against former invasions of their rights, should now so tamely see themselves sold in their elections of representatives, by the worst and lowest of mankind, to him alone that is only more despicable.

During the last elections, instead of preventing the ruin of their country, or lamenting its forlorn condition; the whole attention was taken up about the two tryals, of an old beggar-woman, and an infamous young girl. It recall'd to my mind the state of the Athenian people in the time of Demosthenes, and the pictures he has given of them in his philipics.

Whatever be the event of its present condition, I am not gifted with the art of divination, sufficient to penetrate; but at present it resembles those insects, which are near the moment of a new metamorphosis; but whether an eagle or a moth, a creature that shall face the sun, or be doom'd to perpetual darkness only, a few years must discover, as it is at this hour it cannot long remain.

I am yours most affectionately.

LETTER XXV.

To the Reverend Father ANGELO BONCARO at Rome.

Dear Sir,

THE various sects which fill this isle, resemble the ark of Noah in every thing but one; they are almost as numerous as the whole race of living things, but some of them scarce seem to be of God's creation.

IF they must be imputed to that cause, they seem rather to shew us the excellency of some by the depravity of others, as vice exhibits virtue in its fullest glory, a storm endears the hours of sunshine, or an earthquake enhances the value of the steady course of nature.

METHINKS christianity has been tax'd by the men of pretended reason, with a fault, which in fact ought to have been consider'd as an excellency by them; from its promulgation have sprung as many different sects, as philosophies

from

LETTER XXV.

from that which was call'd reason; should not this analogy have made the enquirers into truth and nature, as it is call'd, determine in its favour rather than the contrary, and have won them to its party, rather than driven them to the opposite; resemblance in other things, generally creates esteem where we have liked one before: In this however it makes an objection.

OF all the opinions that seem to prevail in this nation, that which is reckon'd the most abstruse and deep, is that of fatality, and the most readily adapted, for reasons which may be easily suggested.

IF I should enter into a thorough disquisition on this subject, it would carry me too far for the limits of a letter; besides, I have no other intent at present than to remark, that there is in the human mind, a power of examining, comparing, and combining ideas, which is not in machines; and that if all actions spring from fatality, yet there is something in the fatality of one, which is not to be seen in the fatality of the other. Otherwife there feems to be no more excellence in Homer than in a clock; the mind of the firſt from internal ſprings and weights, or other material cauſes, as neceſſarily points to the thoughts, which combined, make ſuch charming pictures to the reader's imagination, as the latter does to the hour, and the man ſpeaks as mechanically at ſpeaking time, as the clock does at the revolution of the hours at ſtriking time; whence do we admire the fatality in one, and not the other, if each is equally fatal?

IF this be true, it really feems odd that it ſhould; however, if we ſuppoſe all is mechaniſm and neceſſity, we muſt yet accede to this, that this machine has a power of combining, ſeparating, comparing, and diſtinguiſhing ideas, and of examining its own powers, which is not to be found in thoſe of the human contrivance. This no fatalift can deny, and perhaps theſe faculties will probably amount to ſomething adequate to the idea of freedom.

THAT

LETTER XXV.

THAT man should be acquainted with his own fabric, is a thing that cannot be denied by any-one, if he intends to regulate his motions at all.

THIS system of fatality then, tends to make man unacquainted with his own powers; it not only destroys as far as it influences all moral and religious motives, but effaces the knowledge of ourselves. Philosophers in this system proceed no farther, than that every effect has its cause, and therefore every thing is necessary; that as prescience must be an attribute of the deity, prescience includes a certainty of all things being determined as they are, or there can be no prescience; therefore a fatality decides in all things. Here their philosophy rests, considering all things as predestined; thus growing inactive they search no farther into the composition and operation of this machine: does not this tend to destroy the very knowledge of human kind? It cannot be denied, I think, that we have a power of examining ourselves; this makes part of fatality then, if all is fatal.

LETTER XXV.

LET us for once conceive that every faculty of the mind acts mechanically, as in a machine which is kept going by weights and springs; the paſſions are the weights and ſprings which put it in motion, reaſon the pendulum, which balances and corrects the force of the former, and regulates its movements; beſides theſe, that the ſenſes, faith, imagination, and all the large family of the various faculties, have their cauſes to put them into action, and that there is in ſome minds a power of examining all; in this, man differs at leaſt, from the machines of man's invention.

As in the ſtudy of mechanics, the perſon who beſt knows the powers of ſprings, weights, wheels, and levers, and the reſult which follows their combination, will certainly be the moſt expert machinic; and he who has never applied to this ſtudy will have infinite difficulties to ſurmount, in the making the leaſt inſtrument of a complex nature; yet each under the ſame power of neceſſity:

So

So in like manner the philosopher, tho' a fatalist, who intends making any progress in the knowledge of the human mind, should attempt the discovering those objects which influence and affect every part of it, and not rest in the lazy inattentive state of fatality, without enquiring into the motives which set the different parts of this various machine into motion.

In the construction of watches and clocks, he that knows that the elasticity of steel renders it fit for making springs, that it will re-act after being acted upon, that a swinging weight will regulate these motions, has gained already two the most essential parts towards the fabricating these machines; when he finds also, that different powers of the spring make watches go faster or slower; that length of pendulum influences greatly in the motions of a clock, tho' all these differences are found by experience to be so many fatalities, yet, after they are known, he makes a more certain use of them, than if they were not so, and applies all these properties to his own advantage; and tho' influenced by necessity, has a faculty of combining these powers.

In like manner, a fatalist, I mean a philosopher, who knows the mind of man, and how it is affected, should apply the motives which influence the various faculties of the soul; those things which act necessarily according to his scheme, on our hopes, fears, and other passions; faith should have its proper objects to direct it right; the senses be influenced in like manner, operating for the general good; the imagination be affected by the dazzle and delight of future glory; and lastly, the esoteric doctrine should be that of reason, not that limited view of these philosophers at present, which excludes all the parts we have already mentioned, sense, faith, passions and imagination, from their system, as if they contained nothing true; but that of knowing and acknowledging that all things are true, to those faculties which apprehend them, and that the only right reason is that, which conceiving man thus formed, and allowing things to be thus constituted, goes along with the stream of nature in the conduct of the world, acknowledging all these

LETTER XXV.

parts to make the whole of man, and enter into the reason of the universe.

NECESSITY taken in this way would have, in its effect, little difference from free-will and liberty; perhaps, tho' philosophers see it not in this view, this is the way nature proceeds; and on this plan a philosopher would form his system of governing mankind, if he was truly instructed in the knowledge of that fatality he pretended to understand.

THE man who truly comprehends the nature of his own existence, would destine to every part of the soul its proper object, and forming the exactest computation of the powers of all the faculties of the mind, not as they stand in himself, but in all nature as far as he could penetrate, adapt the objects fitted to each perception, and proportioned to the degrees of them in all nature. To the lowest understandings as well as the highest, that each might find its object and influence in governing and regulating the actions of mankind,

FAITH,

LETTER XXV.

Faith, so natural to men of all capacities, especially the meanest, the million, must be fixed on proper objects; the passions animated by particular circumstances, or restrained by others in the articles of belief; the senses awakened and touched by the visible representations of their creed; the mind induced to consider highly of the power believed in, by pomp and worship, and tokens of reverence and gratitude; the weakness of human nature indulged in the hopes of a redeemer and mediator, between a soul sunk to nothing by its vices in its own consideration, and that being of their worship all purity and perfection; the imagination warmed by the objects of another world, combining the whole sum of mental pleasures and supreme delights; and lastly, reason should behold all these right in nature, as wheels, weights, springs, and their powers are in machines, with no greater proof of the truth of the last, than of the first, experience only; which teaches us that these are natural to man, without which sagaciously adjusted, he can no more be governed and go

right,

LETTER XXV.

right, than a clock can measure time. Christianity certainly embraces the whole system of truth to mental nature, necessary if the fatalist pleases, proceeding from the will of God, in the opinion of those who acknowledge a free-will; but in both manners of considering it, equally true with all other things, and equally adapted to our well-being, as rain and sunshine to fruit and flowers.

Thus, Sir, I have been led I know not how into this metaphysical research, to shew you that the system of fatality, as it is generally received, tends to destroy the knowledge of men, and would effect it, if even necessity in all the faculties did not lay claim to its right; fatality in the hands of a man of genius would then be directed much to the same purposes, with those of a man who acknowledged the doctrine of free-will: let me tell you, that the philosophers of England are extremely deficient in this system; they allow that all exists from necessity, and yet, that religion is a false and destructive institution, when this must have the same title to be right and true, with all the most favourite truths of their reason and system; its springing from some cause

LETTER XXV.

cause which is necessary, and it has always made part of the system of nature and government of men; thus, their philosophy and neglect of their religion, tend alike at present to the ruin of national government. I am,

Your most obedient.

LETTER XXVI.

To the Countess of ***** *at* Rome.

Madam,

WHAT you have been told with respect to the English ladies, and women in general, is true; they have an external neatness in their dress, which is to be seen in no other nation upon earth; that part of apparel which is called an apron, unknown to your country, and which I know no way of describing to you, but by referring you, like a mathematician to his diagram, to that little jointed baby which I send you with this, by Mr.———. This figure is drest in the night-gown of England, which being often white, handkerchiefs and caps, as you will see, all of the same hue, give an air of cleanliness beyond imagination.

THIS dress, with their hats on in the public walks, communicates to a stranger the most pleasing sensation, a kind of pastoral delight, a

LETTER XXVI.

scene of old Arcadia, or like some of Wattcau's pictures in the rural kind.

IN Paris the women have quite another air in their motions, looks, dress, and behaviour, they impart a grace of a very superior nature, such as becomes persons of the highest rank in the species; in London, the women of quality have much of the shepherdess mein, or rather inclining to something less modest, the nymphs of the town; this air I presume these ladies affect for a moral purpose, that by this artifice all kinds of characters in women looking alike, the men shall be afraid to accost any of them, lest peradventure, they should meet a virtuous woman and be rejected with contempt. Thus the dames of avowed pleasure are prevented from exerting all their mischief, by being mixt with and undistinguishable from those of professed virtue, as the same quantity of poison diffused thro' a large mass of matter, is less likely to kill, than in its unmixed state; or, wine less apt to intoxicate when it is diffused in water, than when taken alone; this policy you must allow to be admirable in favour of virtue and chastity, amongst the ladies of England.

LETTER XXVI.

Yet I am afraid, madam, that in dress, the same objection lies against the ladies of London, that they say lies against the religion of the Italians; the external show and parade may be greater, but the parts concealed are more neglected, than in the regions of Italy.

A man of my character and function, must be supposed to speak all this from hearsay only, and not knowledge; and I assure you, the gentlemen who have visited the kingdoms on the the other side of the Alps, tell me, that the hidden corners are kept cleaner by our ladies, than by those of England, and internal purity makes ample amends for external appearance.

This I think, is but reasonable in those ladies, if they were as elegantly neat beneath as above, they would like so many Calypsos charm all mankind, and confine them to this island; but they are moderate in their desires, and cherish some hidden disgust on purpose not to dispeople other realms, or, at least, make them all so many nations of Amazons without a man amongst them.

The

LETTER XXVI.

THE persons of English women are certainly very fine, their complexions, shapes, and proportions very pleasing and attractive; yet they are extremely deficient, not only in that which I have already mentioned, but in another internal consideration; they do not give their minds all that beauty, which grace adds to sentiment, and are infinitely less pleasing in conversation, than the ladies of Italy or France.

THUS, tho' they easily captivate, their chains are too feeble to hold their captives long in dependance; they think of no more than the moments of delight, and leave the hours of indifference unprovided for, that is, they decorate their persons, and neglect their understandings.

THUS it happens, that when possession has stript the veil, which love throws over all parts of its objects, unless those destined for the eye; a new scene appears, and all the undiscovered parts of person, in mind and disposition, now put into the opposite scale, weigh down the former, which like gold becomes lighter by wearing.

IT

LETTER XXVI.

IT is to this neglect in England also, that the ladies of France and Italy find such praises in the mouths of English travellers; indeed it is owing to a false notion in this nation, of supposing women unfit for conversation, that it has so long prevailed; whereas, in truth, their understandings are as good as those of the ladies of any nation, and the conversation as brilliant, of all those who have been bred to the use and exertion of their faculties.

THE chief reason that women are less esteemed here than in France, is, that the education of youth tends naturally to keep them from their company; from school they go to the universities, the law, or physic, and are under the tuition of men till three or four and twenty; whereas, a young gentleman in France comes from the college at thirteen or fourteen, and is immediately delivered over to the care and superintendency of some woman of quality, practised in the ways of love, men, and gallantry.

HERE he learns every qualification necessary to accomplish a young gentleman, for the supreme

LETTER XXVI.

preme art and myfteries of love; he is inftructed in all the falacies and deceits of women; the artifices and devices of men; the whole attack and defence of the fex; when being accomplifh'd, he is let loofe, not to make war, but love, on the females of Paris.

From this it is, that the gentlemen of France always think ladies the moft defireable companions for converfation, and the women are ftill inftructed by teaching, as preceptors become more expert by having pupils.

A woman in England is the momentary toy of paffion. In France the companion, in the hours of reafon and converfation, as well as in thofe of love; the fentimental makes the greateft part of the delight: a female of France would blufh at the gothic joys which an Englifhman only thinks of, and pretend at leaft to fly his arms and converfation.

In truth, they fupply the void of love with much art; and if they do not fofter a genuine paffion, they fupport an artificial one fo perfectly,

fectly, that all seems easy and natural. A woman in England, in general, scorns disguise; she will have the whole heart, or nothing; and detests the ghost of a lover, as every thing is call'd but flesh and blood. Indeed the most polite men and their wives have learnt to be civil of late, without caring six-pence for each other. To recompence the loss of these qualities, however amiable, it must be avow'd that virtue is the due praise of English wives; and were the men half so steady to their country's good, as their ladies are to their honor, no nation could boast more illustrious natives.

WITHOUT doubt there are fewer corrupt married woman in this nation, than in any in Europe where women have so much liberty; and husbands have justly more reliance on them, than in any other country. Confidence creates honor, and the liberty of choosing those they love has preserved their virtue; but the time approaches, and the law is talk'd of, which must in some time bring them on a level in levity with other women of Europe: it is determined, that neither honor in man, nor virtue in woman, shall be longer encouraged in this isle; that since the naturalization of the off-cast of all nations cannot take place at present, the expulsion of every virtue may, in order to pave the road for that glorious design. In all probability, madam, a few years, if a law which restrains young people from being wedded to their choices, should be pass'd, the English ladies may be as remarkable for having as much cleanliness, and as little chastity, as those of Italy or any other country.

Their gallantries and intrigues may make them as sentimental, and refined, as either the French or Italians; and the loss of one virtue, (indeed it is a capital one) be amply recompenced by the acquisition of five hundred hypocrisies. This is a thing to be dreaded by the women of all other nations: if beauty makes the females of England already a formidable rival to the French power in that particular, in opposition to internal cleanliness, spirit of conversation, cajoling, and intrigue; what will it effect when it has acquired all these powerful additions?

I TREM-

LETTER XXVI.

I TREMBLE for the continent, and verily believe, that this which appears a design of extirpating female virtue, is in truth a deep-laid scheme to conquer the French in their own way, and declaring a new kind of war, where the powers are female.

IN what a strange light do vulgar eyes behold things! how often are ministers calumniated by the tongue of malice and malediction! what can shew the genius of a statesman to so much advantage, as this single stroke in policy, if it takes place? where, after having exhausted the nation's treasure fruitlessly in war, and mortgaged its honest inhabitants to public plunderers, he discovers a new way of raising the reputation of his country, by abolishing all female honor as much as he can, on purpose to oppose the gallantries, intrigues, and adulteries of this nation, against those of France, and thus beat them at their own weapons in a new kind of war. I am told, by this he expects to be as much famed for spreading the powers of vice every where, and conquering the virtues of both sexes,

LETTER XXVI.

as the Duke of Marlborough was renown'd for subduing the enemies of the crown of England. Alas! I tremble for the grand monarch. I am,

Madam,

*Your most obedient,
and most humble servant,*

End of the FIRST VOLUME.

www.ingramcontent.com/pod-product-compliance
Lightning Source LLC
Chambersburg PA
CBHW032051230426
43672CB00009B/1560